◇◇◇

VIRGINIA WOOLF

Manly Johnson

BIP 88

Frederick Ungar Publishing Co.
New York

Second Printing, 1978

Copyright © 1973 by Frederick Ungar Publishing Co., Inc.
Printed in the United States of America
Library of Congress Catalog Card Number: 72-79944
Designed by Anita Duncan
ISBN: 0-8044-2424-1 (cloth)

VIRGINIA WOOLF

Modern Literature Monographs

For MARY

To cure the work of Time it is necessary to "go back" and find the "beginning of the world."

MIRCEA ELIADE, *Myth and Reality*

Contents

Chronology

1878: Leslie Stephen and Julia Jackson Duckworth are married.

1882: Adeline Virginia Stephen born, 26 March, at 22 Hyde Park Gate, London.

1895: Death of Julia Stephen. Virginia has first nervous breakdown.

1897: Stella Duckworth, stepsister, dies. Virginia ill. Begins to study Greek at King's College.

1899: Brother Thoby enters Cambridge, with Clive Bell, Lytton Strachey, and Leonard Woolf.

1902: Takes private lessons in Greek. Has close friendship with Violet Dickinson.

1904: Death of Leslie Stephen after long illness. Virginia's second serious mental illness. Moves to 46 Gordon Square, Bloomsbury. Visits Italy and France. First publication, a review in *The Guardian*. Leonard Woolf to Ceylon as a government administrator.

1905: Visits Spain and Portugal with brother Adrian for two weeks.

1906: Visits Greece. Thoby Stephen dies of typhoid at 26. Virginia writes to Violet Dickinson (ill with typhoid) for a month, pretending Thoby still alive.

1907: Moves with Adrian to 29 Fitzroy Square. Begins work on first novel.

1908: Visits Italy. Julian, a first child, is born to Vanessa (Virginia's sister) and Clive Bell.

1909: Proposal of marriage from Lytton Strachey, accepted. He breaks it off. Receives a legacy of £ 2500. Visits Italy; Bayreuth for Wagner festival.

1910: Ill through the summer. Takes rest cure in nursing home. Birth of Vanessa's second child, Quentin. Roger Fry organizes first Post-Impressionist exhibition.

1911: Brief visit to Turkey. Leonard Woolf returns from Ceylon.

1912: Rest cure in nursing home. Leonard Woolf proposes. They marry, 10 August, honeymoon in France, Spain, and Italy. Lease Asham House until 1919.

1913: Completes *The Voyage Out*, first novel. Increasing illness, rest cure in nursing home. Leonard Woolf advised Virginia should not have children. Attempts suicide by overdose of veronal.

1915: Move to Hogarth House, Paradise Road, Richmond (there until 1924). Violent illness, in nursing home. Publication by Gerald Duckworth of *The Voyage Out*.

1916: Early work on second novel, *Night and Day*.

1917: Printing press in Hogarth House. First publications: *The Mark on the Wall* (Virginia), *Three Jews* (Leonard). Begins diary, portions to be published in 1953 as *A Writer's Diary*. Writing for *The Times Literary Supplement*.

1918: Working on *Night and Day*. Reads manuscript of Joyce's *Ulysses*. First meeting with T. S. Eliot. *Kew Gardens* published. Frequent visits with

Katherine Mansfield. Birth of Vanessa's third child, Angelica.

1919: Prints Eliot's *Poems*. Give up Asham House. Purchase and move to Monk's House, Rodmell, Sussex.

1920: Begins *Jacob's Room*.

1921: *Monday or Tuesday* published. Lytton Strachey's *Queen Victoria*.

1922: Ill health. *Jacob's Room* published. Meets Mrs. Harold Nicolson (Vita Sackville-West).

1923: Katherine Mansfield dies. Leonard becomes literary editor of *The Nation*. Visit to Spain and France. At work on *Mrs. Dalloway*.

1924: Move to 52 Tavistock Square, Bloomsbury (houses the Press until 1939). *Mrs. Dalloway* completed. *Mr. Bennett and Mrs. Brown* published.

1925: *The Common Reader* and *Mrs. Dalloway* published.

1926: At work on *To the Lighthouse*.

1927: *To the Lighthouse* published. Frequent visits with Vita Sackville-West. Begins *Orlando*.

1928: Awarded *Femina Vie Heureuse* prize. *Orlando* published. Visits France with Vita Sackville-West. Reads two papers to the women's colleges at Cambridge.

1929: Trip to Germany. *A Room of One's Own* (the Cambridge lectures) published. At work on *The Waves*.

1931: *The Waves* published.

1932: *A Letter to a Young Poet* and *The Common Reader: Second Series* published.

1933: Refuses an honorary doctorate. Trip to France. At work on *The Years*. Declines Leslie Stephen lectureship at Cambridge. *Flush* published.

1934:   Continues work on *The Years*. *Walter Sickert: A Conversation* published.

1936:   At work on *Three Guineas*. Collecting material for *Roger Fry*.

1937:   *The Years* published. Julian Bell killed in Spanish Civil War.

1938:   Sells interest in Hogarth Press to John Lehmann. At work on *Roger Fry*. *Three Guineas* published.

1939:   Meets Sigmund Freud. Refuses an honorary doctorate. Visits France.

1940:   Reads paper in Brighton to Workers' Educational Association (later published as "The Leaning Tower"). *Roger Fry: A Biography* published.

1941:   Completes *Between the Acts*. Ill. Drowns herself in river not far from Monk's House. *Between the Acts* published.

For a detailed chronology, the reader should consult Quentin Bell's biography of Virginia Woolf.

1

$$\diamond$$

Life,

Essays,

Biographies

She transmits it and makes us share it;
but it is always by her means,
in her language, with her susceptibility,
and not ours.
That is why she is so tantalising,
so original, and so satisfying.

Few have prepared as thoroughly for a vocation as Virginia Stephen Woolf, who decided as a child to become a writer. She learned how to work from watching her father's steady application that produced several articles a week; she had access to his well-stocked library that her own feminist resentment motivated her to use with diligence. And when she was ready to begin her career, in her middle twenties, a small inheritance made her independent. During the early years when she was writing about literature in reviews and essays, and beginning her first novel, she was fortunate in being surrounded by some of the most stimulating minds of her generation.

Since excellent sources for the life of Virginia Woolf are available, the purpose of the following biographical details is to bring out those aspects of her experience that lead to the view of life and art appearing in the essays and novels. Among the most important influences were those of her parents and husband.

Her father, Leslie Stephen, began his professional life as a clergyman and tutor at Cambridge, but within a few years became thoroughly agnostic, left the Church and took up journalism. He produced a monumental *History of English Thought in the Eighteenth Century*, several studies in the *English Men of Letters* series, and *Science and Ethics*. He edited the *Cornhill Magazine* for a decade, and devoted years to editing the *Dictionary of National Biography*.

Noel Annan, in his fine critical study of Stephen, observes that he can be properly understood only in the context of his place in the nineteenth century aristocracy of intellect. For the life of Virginia Woolf, his significance lies in her sense of belonging by birth to that aristocracy and, as corollary, the need to resist being dominated by her father's personality.

His domestic style had much to do with her resentment of male tyranny. He appears to have tried running his home in much the same way that he coached a rowing crew at Cambridge. Only his being "the most lovable of men" (his friend James Russell Lowell's opinion, which Virginia Woolf in a 1932 essay quotes with approval) kept him from being intolerable—that and his genuine sense of mission, almost always overlooked in unsympathetic commentaries about his portrait as Mr. Ramsay in *To the Lighthouse.*

Virginia's mother, Julia, also appears in that novel as Mrs. Ramsay. In her diary on what would have been her father's ninety-sixth birthday, Virginia recalled being "obsessed by them both, unhealthily." In the second marriage for each, Leslie and Julia had four children, of which the third, born in 1882, was Virginia. Julia Stephen was generous with her advice when it was sought—as it often was—and selfless in responding to pleas for counsel and comfort. But she also had a managerial bent, was a matchmaker, and a firm critic of young Virginia's contributions to the children's domestic newsletter, *The Hyde Park Gate News.* It was to free herself from the domination of these two overpowering personalities—"to lay the ghosts of mother and father"—that Virginia wrote *To the Lighthouse.*

In Virginia Stephen's compulsive drive to work, evidently acquired from her parents, and the strain it placed on a constitution too frail for such demands, lies part of the answer to her unstable health. Though clinical causes of her mental illness are not known, several circumstances aggravated her condition. Quentin Bell's biography presents a catalogue of horrors—repeated shocks to a hypersensitive, emotionally unstable young girl.

What a biographer cannot do, having to "stick to the facts," is to show the inner resources that are marshaled to withstand the pressure of traumatic events. Since, in the case of Virginia Stephen, the inner resources were eventually disciplined and directed toward producing the novels, it is the novels that provide a salutary corrective to the sometimes morbid and depressing data about her external life.

The following outline of the sensational events surrounding her childhood—especially madness and aberrant sexuality—are offered with the caveat that they are not true, that is, not the whole truth. For that we turn to the novels.

Laura, Stephen's child from his first marriage, had succumbed to the insanity that dominated her grandmother, Mrs. William Makepeace Thackeray. But Laura was kept in the Stephen family, startling the children from time to time with her wildly eccentric conduct. More disturbing to Virginia were the consequences of a head injury to her brilliant cousin, a man in his twenties, J. K. Stephen, who became increasingly demented until his death six years later. During that time (Virginia's fourth to tenth years) he developed an insane passion for Stella Duckworth, Julia Stephen's daughter from her first marriage, invading the Stephen house in Hyde Park Gate in pursuit of her, until his death in 1892 brought the inroads to a halt.

In 1895, Julia Stephen died. Looking back on it, Virginia described her mother's death as "the greatest disaster that could have happened." A few weeks later Virginia, then thirteen, had her first serious mental breakdown. There was perhaps some guilt associated with a sense of having somehow "rejected" her mother in an early childhood choice of her father as favorite parent. Contributing to her deep depression during the next years was Leslie Stephen's excessive and histrionic mourning.

Virginia's stepsister, Stella Duckworth, died two years later. When Stella had assumed their mother's duties in the Stephen household, dissension developed between her and Virginia. During the prolonged illness leading to Stella's death, Virginia also became ill—coincidence perhaps, but perhaps also a recurrence of the response to her mother's death, with its shadow of guilt.

Most troubling to Virginia, especially in conjunction with mental illness, was the relationship with her stepbrother, George Duckworth, the oldest of Julia's children from her first marriage, already fourteen when Virginia was born. We are not left to speculate about the nature of his attentions, for in the last year of her life she wrote to a friend recalling her shame, when she was six, at being fondled by George. Incidents of this kind continued to occur until Virginia was in her early twenties.

The effect on her is impossible to determine, but it is suggested in *The Voyage Out* by Rachel's nightmare after being passionately embraced by the husband of a shipboard acquaintance. A voice moans for her, and barbaric men snuffle at her door. Rachel's revulsion and fascination are like young Virginia's response to her demented cousin's pursuit of Stella and the molestations of her stepbrother.

Experiences of this kind explain in part Virginia Stephen's preference early in life for women as objects of her affection and love, and later for her willingness to entertain the possibility of marrying Lytton Strachey, a homosexual. That way she might obtain the benefits of intellectual companionship without the male-associated brutality of sex. But the more she saw of men the more she realized that the difficulty was not just sexuality: "I think what an abrupt precipice cleaves asunder the male intelligence, and how they pride themselves on a point of view that much resembles stupidity."

In her teens, she fervently admired women like Madge Vaughan (daughter of John Addington Symonds) who wrote novels. She is pictured as the extroverted Sally Seton in *Mrs. Dalloway.*[1] In middle life, Virginia was much attracted to Vita Sackville-West, also a writer and woman of strong, independent spirit. She was fascinated by Vita's dark, full-breasted beauty, her air of authority, and impressed by Knole, the great country house, and Vita's aristocratic forebears.

The nature of Virginia's feeling can be seen in her similar fascination with a quite different kind of woman, the writer Katherine Mansfield. She and Vita were both worked into *Orlando* in a vicarious display of all that Virginia was not, and envied—the worldly assurance, spontaneity, promiscuousness, and exoticism, as they appear in Sasha, the Muscovite princess; in Lolita, the gypsy dancer; in Orlando, familiar of prostitutes; and in the bisexual Archduchess Harriet Griselda.

She was herself attractive to men, as demonstrated by courtship and several proposals of marriage. The attentions of her brother-in-law, Clive Bell, Vanessa's husband, continued over a decade, making its own contribution to Virginia's strained emotional life. Irregular emotional entanglements with men (who, it appeared to her, were free to do as they liked) fed

Virginia Stephen's resentment of male domination.

Under the exactions and restrictions of her father's beneficent tyranny, she began early to acquire for herself the education that exclusion from the man's world of the universities denied her. But it would be incorrect to interpret Virginia's early attempts to educate herself in her father's library and train herself for writing as wholly the result of a grievance.

Her great novels sprang largely from a positive impulse, not a negative, and the source of that impulse rose in her earliest years:

Between or behind the dense and involved confusion which grown-up life presented there appeared for moments chinks of pure daylight in which the simple, unmistakable truth, the underlying reason, otherwise so overlaid and befogged, was revealed.[2]

Though the malign influence of disturbing events in her childhood on the future course of her life cannot be denied, they were the dark within which the light of purpose was already glowing. What Virginia Woolf goes on to say about W. H. Hudson is applicable also to her: "The little boy whom he remembers was already set with even fresher passion upon the same objects that Mr Hudson has sought all his life.

Though her father's death apparently freed her to begin a life of her own, it was delayed. Within months of Leslie Stephen's death in 1904, she suffered her second serious mental breakdown, this time complicated by scarlet fever and attempted suicide. Recovering, she was finally able to enter a world where she could be relatively independent.

Virginia had lived hardly two years in a Bloomsbury house, with Vanessa and their brothers Thoby and Adrian, before Thoby died of typhoid fever. He

was her alter ego—inheritor of all wisdom at Cambridge and free to roam the world (his role in *Jacob's
Room*), a hero dead before his time (as Percival in
The Waves). Then with Vanessa married, and Adrian
so much younger as not to count, Virginia was at last
on her own.

She had only moved from the Stephen family circle into a somewhat larger circle of intellectual associ-
ates. But it was a liberating environment. Thoby had
introduced several of his Cambridge friends to the
house in Bloomsbury, where the first of those later to
be known as the Bloomsbury group met to talk about
art and ideas—such men as novelist E. M. Forster,
economist John Maynard Keynes, poet and biographer
Lytton Strachey, and art critic Clive Bell. In this group
Virginia Stephen knew the energizing intellectual life
("when mind prints upon mind indelibly") that she
describes in *Jacob's Room*.

They formed a heterogeneous group, but all under
the personal influence of the Cambridge don G. E.
Moore. Moore's *Principia Ethica* had such impact,
wrote Leonard Woolf, that it "passed into our unconscious." But Moore's devotion to truth could only rein-
force in Virginia the imperatives received from her
father: "To read what one liked because one liked it,
never to pretend to admire what one did not," and "To
write in the fewest possible words, as clearly as possible, exactly what one meant."[3]

The originality of her "vision" (as it has come to
be called, as opposed to a philosophical position,
which she did not have) illustrates the point made by
another of the group, Leonard Woolf, that Bloomsbury
productions were "purely individual"—whether Key-
nesian economics, Fry's "significant form," or Virginia
Woolf's view of life.[4]

But Bloomsbury had a double influence, reflected in the social gatherings so important in her novels. As a coterie, the group afforded a protective environment in which (1) the play of wit and ideas stimulated her intellect, and (2), a community of feeling helped to alleviate her intermittent despair. In *Mrs. Dalloway*, Clarissa's impulse to self-isolation and suicide is dissipated in the midst of a spirited gathering of friends; and in *The Years* life's ugliness and perversions are included and transformed in the human association of an all-night party. In that novel, the party of the Pargiter clan is so unequivocally the party of us all, that warm good feeling is implied as possible therapy for the world at large.

Yet for Virginia Stephen personally, perhaps because of her illness, the amorphous geniality of social intercourse was not sufficient. She needed personal involvement from day to day, someone to stabilize her volatile moods. In Leonard Woolf, one of her brother Thoby's Cambridge friends, she found what she needed. They had met casually, and a deeper relationship did not develop until his return in 1911 from seven years as a government administrator in Ceylon. They were married the following year. Virginia was to find in him a combination of qualities ideal for her—intellectual brilliance, patience, emotional stability, firmness.

He protected his wife when she was well and took care of her when she was ill. Without his constant solicitude she very probably would have carried out earlier one of the several attempts to end her life. Her feeling for him in this role is probably best exemplified in the healthy personality of Lucrezia, the Italian wife of the insane Septimus Smith, described in *Mrs. Dalloway* as being like the tree of life; and in René, the

Frenchman, whose warm, happy marriage is depicted with evident affection in *The Years*. The exotic (non-British) qualities of these two reflect the exotic in Leonard Woolf, a Jew.

But beyond his tireless solicitude, Leonard made contributions to her stock of ideas and her values. He established the musical atmosphere of their home, and her diary makes frequent reference to her reliance on his literary judgment. From the beginning he made their marriage a partnership.

The founding of the Hogarth Press (in 1917) resulted from his concern for Virginia's health. He hoped that the manual work of setting type and binding copies would calm her mental activity. Unfortunately for this objective, the very success of the enterprise necessitated having the work done by others. Yet it was convenient to be able to publish their own work. More importantly for Virginia, reading manuscripts supplemented reviewing to keep her acquainted with contemporary writing.

In this way she had an early look at Joyce's *Ulysses*. She did not like the book's tone, but would have been willing to publish it. They could not themselves undertake so large a job, and other printers they sought, fearing legal action, would not touch it. Among the authors published by the Hogarth Press during Virginia's time were: W. H. Auden, Ivan Bunin, T. S. Eliot, E. M. Forster, Sigmund Freud, Roger Fry, Maksim Gorky, Robert Graves, Christopher Isherwood, Maynard Keynes, Harold Laski, Day Lewis, Katherine Mansfield, Edwin and Willa Muir, J. Middleton Murry, Mussolini, William Plomer, Herbert Read, Rainer Maria Rilke, Alice Ritchie, Vita Sackville-West, Edith Sitwell, Italo Svevo, Chekov, Tolstoy, and H. G.

Wells. Virginia's official connection with the Hogarth Press ended in 1938, when she sold her half interest to John Lehmann, who had earlier for a year been manager of the Press.

Leonard Woolf perhaps thought that a project such as the Hogarth Press, so close to Virginia's own professional interests, might receive the devotion she would have given to the children she could not have. During her third serious breakdown, after the completion of *The Voyage Out* in 1913, Leonard had been advised that Virginia should not bear children. As a consequence, the two bestowed their affections on each other and their friends, and gave their energies to their work.

Having no children of her own, Virginia devoted considerable attention to those of her brother and sister. She was at ease with children and they with her. She drew them out because she wanted to hear experiences. The persistence of her questioning indicates that she was, like Wordsworth, trying to recapture the fresh, curious outlook of the young, and "the unmistakable truth, the underlying reason," that children occasionally glimpse. She might, with Wordsworth, believe that "the child is father of the man," and wish her days "bound each to each by natural piety." But her skepticism would permit only the qualified optimism of Nicholas in *The Years*—that Mankind itself is in its infancy.

And her agnosticism would not allow her any formulated faith in an afterlife, though Vita Sackville-West recalled that once she spoke with deep seriousness about immortality and personal survival after death. Instead of faith in an afterlife distinct from the life of this world, she believed in a process of imaginative discovery, which was in effect a refusal to accept anything in place of life. Exploration, discovery, examination—these were ways to extend life.

For her, the work of the imagination was to weave a kind of tapestry against death, like that of Penelope to hold off her unwanted suitors. She could weave in words, for instance, the idea of a tree and its death: how in life it was a mystery, and in a storm felled. "Even so, life isn't done with." And then she patiently unweaves its death, thinking of wood in chests of drawers, planks, and paneling: "there are a million patient, watchful lives still for a tree, all over the world, in bedrooms, in ships . . . lining rooms, where men and women sit after tea, smoking cigarettes."[5]

Her refusal to accept anything but life led her, in each story, in each novel, to construct intricate relationships between the impersonal world ("which is a proof of existence other than ours") and people. Having observed the death of a tree in the impersonal world and followed its visible dispersion into new forms of existence, she brings these new forms into relationship with the personal world. The analogy is clear: what occurs in an existence other than ours may occur also in ours.

The life of Virginia Woolf presents many parallels to the course of civilization in the twentieth century: early promise, great achievement, interrupted by periods of instability and madness, and the impulse to self-destruction. Her writing is the record of attempts to understand the paradoxes within herself. A major tenet of her thought—that the sanity of one depends on the sanity of all—was directed through her writing toward helping her fellows avoid the fate overtaking her own life.

In the early spring of 1941, her mental illness became more severe. She felt that this time she could not recover. "I have fought against it but can't any longer." She would not go on "spoiling" her husband's life. At noon one day in March, she walked to the river not far from their house in Rodmell, Sussex, and drowned herself.[6]

Despite illness, Virginia Woolf produced an impressive amount of expository writing, beginning in 1904 when her first review was published. Her husband records that "What she was writing or going to write was rarely not in the centre of her mind."[7] Concentration of that kind during regular working days of ten to twelve hours helps to account for an output of five volumes of collected essays and reviews, two biographies (*Flush* and *Roger Fry*), the two libertarian books (*A Room of One's Own* and *Three Guineas*), and a volume of selections from her diary, published in 1953 by Leonard Woolf as *A Writer's Diary*—all in addition to the nine novels and a volume of short stories.

An opinion ventured in *Orlando* applies with particular force to her own books: "Every secret of a writer's soul, every experience of his life, every quality of his mind is written large in his works." Yet despite a characteristic quality that marks all her writing, readers divide in preferring the fiction, or the essays and expository books of feminism and biography.

During nearly two decades after publication of her first libertarian book, *A Room of One's Own*, in 1928, more copies of her nonfiction than of fiction were sold. Since the end of World War II more readers have purchased the novels.[8] As to the relative merits of the two kinds of writing, enough opinion has been

offered by both common readers and critics to suggest
that division of preference will continue.

Two writers who knew her first when they were
young men provide typically contrasting views. Poet
and editor John Lehmann declared in his autobiography, "I devoured [the novels] again and again, and
always with fresh delight, valuing them far higher than
*The Common Reader, A Room of One's Own, Or-
lando,* and *Flush.*"[9] But novelist and poet William
Plomer wrote: "I rather diffidently told her how much
I had been impressed by *The Waves* and that I like it
best among her novels. What I didn't tell her was that I
have always preferred *The Common Reader* and its
successors to her fiction."[10] One is tempted to see in
these views of her writing the poles from which some-
day a middle position will be determined. It is more
likely that they indicate temperamental preferences
that will continue to divide readers.

Virginia Woolf herself makes perhaps the essential distinction in "The Art of Biography." The biographer, because he is limited to facts, is tied; the novelist,
bound only by the truth of his vision, is free. So, in
writing the biographical essay, "Leslie Stephen," she
restricted herself to reporting her father's work habits,
his advice, and opinions about him. But in *To the
Lighthouse* she gives us a portrait of her father in Mr.
Ramsay whose authenticity lies in the truth of her vision.

To use her own words about the work of great
novelists, *To the Lighthouse* produces "that high degree of tension which gives us reality." She states it
directly in "The New Biography" (1927): "Truth of
fact and truth of fiction are incompatible; yet [the bi-
ographer] is now more than ever urged to combine
them. For it would seem that the life which is increas-

ingly real to us is the fictitious life; it dwells in the personality rather than in the act."

Thoughts of this kind led Virginia Woolf from her vision of the Stephen family as the Ramsays (1927) to an attempt at combining fact with vision in *Orlando: A Biography* (1928). Many readers find, however much they enjoy its verve and satire, that it lacks the high degree of tension that gives a sense of reality. A few years later she made another attempt in *Flush: A Biography*, which recounts the life of Elizabeth Barrett Browning's dog. In this book, too, despite its charm, Woolf falls under the shadow of her own comment: if the biographer disregards truth, "or can only introduce it with incongruity, he loses both worlds; he has neither the freedom of fiction nor the substance of fact." In *Flush* occur many such passages as this:

Then she would make him stand in front of the looking-glass and asked him why he barked and trembled. Was not the little brown dog opposite himself? But what is "oneself"? Is it the thing people see? Or is it the thing one is?

The personality is human, the acts are those of a dog, which often results in a damaging incongruity—though *Flush* is admirable as a virtuoso piece.

What she means by the distinction between personality and act appears in "Mr. Bennett and Mrs. Brown," her famous dissent from the fictional practices of John Galsworthy, Arnold Bennett, and H. G. Wells. In this essay (1924) she opposes the view of reality taken by three established authors of the time. Wells, looking at the elderly, threadbare Mrs. Brown seated across from him in the railway carriage, would imagine a utopian world in which no Mrs. Browns existed. Galsworthy, looking at her, would seethe with indignation at social injustice in the world. Bennett, says

Woolf, would really look at Mrs. Brown, only to ne-
glect her in noting all the details of dress and the fur-
nishings of the compartment, and thence to a minute
description of the world outside the train. All three
writers laid too much stress on "the fabric of things"
and lost sight of Mrs. Brown, her individuality, her
uniqueness.

But capturing that uniqueness is not simply a matter of technique—it requires vision, by which she
means imaginative insight. Other writers of the time
had vision—such as E. M. Forster and D. H. Law-
rence. But they made the mistake of compromise,
clouding their insight with the representational novelists' myriad facts. Others, such as T. S. Eliot, Joyce,
and Strachey, sincere and courageous, broke through
Edwardian dullness with magnificent experiments, but
dissipated their force in the labor of pioneering. The
essay concludes with Virginia Woolf urging readers to
demand from authors a Mrs. Brown of "unlimited
capacity and infinite variety."

In other essays, she ranges beyond technique and
characterization to more general questions of time and
milieu as they affect literature. In "American Fiction"
she comments on Ring Lardner's interest in games, and
speculates that the baseball park is his equivalent to
the English drawing room, providing rules of conduct
and ethics, even a kind of morality, held in common by
a vast continent of people without the traditions of
established society in England. She extends her observation to account for the inadequacies of Sinclair
Lewis: denied the richness of an old civilization and
the solidity of custom, he was forced to criticize rather
than explore. It was her persisting belief that a novelist's ability to open new territory—to explore and extend human sensibility—is his primary asset.

Of all her nonfiction, A *Writer's Diary* (1953) best exemplifies her exploration in search of the truest way to express her vision of life. Her husband selected the entries about writing from the journals kept from 1915 to 1941. The diary is an account of works in progress, and a record of what she learned from her predecessors in the art of story-telling. As such, it is a professional journal.

But it also logs the private explorations of her personal life—frequently expressing her chagrin at not being on a par with men, and uncertain what the parity should be. Perhaps she never fully escaped the dominance of her father, or learned how to cope with the assurance of university-trained men. "I wobble," she writes, comparing her vacillation with the firmness of Lytton Strachey.

Her feminine libertarianism is most enlightened in those works that recognize the difficulties of arriving at a true assessment of responsibilities in a heterosexual world. She brings these doubts together in 1918 in a review about women novelists. Women cannot—any more than men, she says—free themselves from the tyranny of sex One cannot possibly mistake a novel written by a man for one written by a woman because "each describes itself." She concluded with a generalization about how the two sexes differ over what constitutes the importance of any subject: "From this spring not only marked differences of plot and incident, but infinite differences in selection, method and style."

Most of her writing on this subject, however, is keenly alert to women's subjection. In "American Fiction" (1925) she observes that the sensitivity of women writers to their sex is like that of blacks, "galled by the memory of their chains." The more effective of her book-length works about the suppres-

sion of women is *A Room of One's Own* (1929).
There she develops the metaphor of woman as a looking-glass "possessing the magic and delicious power of
reflecting the figure of man at twice its natural size." If
woman tells the truth, the figure in the looking-glass
begins to shrink. "Take it away and man may die, like
the drug fiend deprived of his cocaine."

Woolf most dramatically illustrated the theme of
this book, however, in the hypothetical story of Shakespeare's gifted sister—as adventurous and imaginative
as her brother. Rather than accept an arranged marriage, Judith Shakespeare runs away to London. She is
attracted to the stage, but as a woman cannot get a job
acting. She frequents the theater until she is made
pregnant by an actor-manager and kills herself. That,
concludes Virginia Woolf, is more or less the way the
story would run.

But, she goes on, the story is absurd: "For genius
like Shakespeare's is not born among labouring, servile, uneducated people." Why expect it then, she asks,
to be born among women, who are also servile and
uneducated? Women of genius will not appear until
they can be independent, have enough to live on, and
possess rooms of their own.

Ways of attaining these goals is the subject of
Three Guineas, her final book of social protest. Appearing in 1938, it reflected the gathering clouds of
war, the inevitable product, in her view, of a male-
dominated exploitive society. The first of her proposals
is an experimental college in which the curriculum
would explore new ways of cooperation between mind
and body. Until such colleges are available, women can
only support the ones we have and refuse, themselves,
to teach "any art or science that encourages war."

She observed that men have always conspired to

keep women out of the professions, citing as their authorities God, Law, and Property. In attacking this position, Woolf invokes a favorite authority of her own —Antigone, daughter of Oedipus. Defying Creon and the Theban state, she paid with her life for the freedom of private judgment.

With the male tyranny of Creon in mind, Woolf employs the Victorian father figure to show the relationship between the private and public mania to dominate. It was a sickness that had a deeply unconscious emotional basis and was a powerful force in combination: fathers "massed together in societies, in professions, were even more subject to the fatal disease than the fathers in private." The male establishment, as paterfamilias, carried on into the twentieth century the deadening work of suppressing women.

But it was met by a force that became strong enough to oppose it. Feminism, the emancipation of women—Virginia Woolf did not like the usual terms because they did not express the real emotions that lay behind women's resistance. "Freedom" is misleading, for it implies license. What women want, like Antigone, is "not to break the laws but to find the law."

The link between domination and war was certain, in her mind. When Creon buried Antigone alive for defying the order of things established by men, he "brought ruin on his house, and scattered the land with the bodies of the dead." The public and the private worlds are indeed one, and the three causes to which she has been asked to contribute a guinea each— women's education, professional equality, and prevention of war—contain both.

Virginia Woolf's pursuit of truth in *Three Guineas* is uncompromising, after the example of the early Bloomsbury group's mentor, G. E. Moore. Though beautifully expressed, analytical and cool, the pursuit leaves one feeling the fanatical dedication of an Antigone: there are no laws but Law.

In her writings about art, Woolf turned from the public world of disorder and catastrophe to the private satisfactions of painting and music. Despite her belief that the public and the private worlds are one, she was clearly more at home in the private. "Walter Sickert: a Conversation" (1934) is her most instructive piece for the connection it has with her fiction. In discussing the effect of Walter Sickert's paintings, she briefly extended the visual to the visionary—a shift of thematic importance in many of the novels, where it is frequently her way of looking at the colorful surface of the world so as to see through it to something beyond.

How soon we lose our sense of color, she remarks, because of the denotative values attached to them: in our time, colors have become hardly more than signals. She recalls hearing about an insect in South America whose body is a mere tuft connecting two great chambers of vision, and another kind that absorbs color until he becomes that color. She wonders, were we insects like these once, and whether the capacity still lies hidden somewhere within us to become what we see. Ages ago we lost "the microscopic eye." When we left the forest the "eye shrivelled" as our other organs grew.

She did not, of course, propose this as a theory of phylogeny, but as a theory of sensibility. A painting may suggest an episode or story, but when the combinations of line and color create an emotion that is "distinct, powerful and satisfactory," we are unable to say what it is. We have been returned to the forest, back to the degree of pure response—what Virginia Woolf calls the "silent land."

She wanted her own art of writing to evoke the powerful, satisfying, nonverbal response that good painting gives, as well as communicate the meaning that can be put into words—she wanted, in short, feeling plus concept. The story—yes, for the medium of her own art was words. But she wanted also to "make us feel something that has nothing to do with the story." Why Virginia Woolf was attracted to this "silent land" appears almost by chance in an introduction to a show of Vanessa Bell's paintings. A canvas of Vanessa's "would go on saying something of its own imperturbably. And perhaps by degrees—who knows? —one would become an inmate of these strange painters' world, in which mortality does not enter, and psychology is held at bay, and there are not words." The "silent land" is attractive not because it is wordless, primarily, but because it is deathless.

In her biography of Roger Fry (1940) she quoted with approval his view that in painting, in music, in literature lay the enduring reality. This biography, the next to last of all the books she wrote, does much to show how "he changed the taste of his time by his writing, altered the current of English painting by his championship of the Post-Impressionists, and increased immeasureably the love of art by his lectures." Yet for all Woolf's enthusiasm for her friend, and for all its accurate rendering of a vital period in English art, the account lacks tension. There is more of vintage Woolf in the eighteen pages of "Walter Sickert" than in all three hundred pages of *Roger Fry*. It was a labor of love, and though the love is apparent, so is the labor. Much like her father's writing in its smooth competence, it has no "moments" that even in her least successful novels produce flickers of lightning.

The conflict between facts and imagination, that

intrudes even into the nonfiction, is ultimately irreconcilable in her writing. To "love life," and to describe that life as physical—as in the thrust of legs, and women giving suck to babes—and to insist that the life "increasingly real to us" dwells in personality, not in acts, is to establish and maintain a paradox.

But it is, after all, this paradox that creates the tension in Virginia Woolf's writing. Her first novel, *The Voyage Out*, is resonant with the possibilities of a voyage in; *Night and Day* is an experiment in infusing opposites with each other; and the last novel, like its title, *Between the Acts*, invokes without false resolution the mysteries that every life is poised between. Virginia Woolf's life of imagination and life of facts do not compete, they complete each other.

Leonard Woolf in the final volume of his autobiography quotes Montaigne: "It is not the arrival, it is the journey which matters." Virginia Woolf's similar commitment to the "process of living" was a commitment to wholeness. All her professional life she looked for a way to represent action in combination with intense emotions. Part of that search resulted in the reviews and essays that record her debt to predecessors.

But the full account of her explorations is found only in the novels, in which as far as possible through words she made an approach to the "silent land" without sacrificing the movement, light, and sounds, of physical reality. In this regard one should observe carefully her diagnosis in "The Leaning Tower" of the social-protest poets of the 1930s: "The inner mind was paralyzed because the surface mind was always hard at work." Given the importance she attached to the work of the inner (subconscious) mind, her desire for the "silent land" was not so much a fear of death, as a fear of incompetence: she could write essays, and she could write the mystical poetry of the vignette "Blue and Green"; but could she write that ideal amalgam referred to in her diary as the Essay-Novel?

2

❖❖

The Voyage Out
and
Night and Day

Have I the power of conveying
the true reality?
Or do I write essays
about myself?

*T*he *Voyage Out* was begun in 1908 and completed in 1913. During that time Virginia Stephen (Woolf from 1912) worked out at least five complete versions of her first novel. Such application would appear to promise a work of unusual complexity. Yet an unwary reader may be lulled into a false sense of the usual by a representational surface and the traditional romantic involvements of a young woman on holiday.

A useful clue to Virginia Woolf's kind of writing is provided by E. M. Forster in discussing prophetic fiction: ". . . as soon as we catch the song in it, it grows difficult and immensely important." The prophetic song sounds early in *The Voyage Out* and makes it in some ways a complex book.

One early October afternoon in London, a man and a woman are walking along the Embankment. They are on their way to board a ship for South America. The woman, Helen Ambrose, observes the gloomy sights around her: the sodden flower woman, the tattered old men and women sleeping on benches, and the endless parade of anonymous figures along the pavement. It is like a scene in some underworld of Dante or Virgil. They take a cab, and as it winds through the streets of London, the short journey from the brilliantly lit West End eastward toward the gloom and odors of the dockside, prepares a reader for the symbolic overtones of the longer expeditions to follow.

At the dockside, a little old man approaches out of the fog and offers to row the unhappy woman and her husband to the ship Euphrosyne (Mirth) at anchor in the channel. As the old man leads the Ambroses to the bottom of a flight of steps at the river's edge, the reader receives an impression that the ferryman in the land of the dead is about to convey two more spirits across the river Styx.

The symbolism is not developed—indeed it is understated—but the odd overtones of the scene remain and sensitize the mind to other elements that soon begin to appear. They are frequently no more than fleeting images or verbal suggestions, as when London, observed from the moving ship at night, appears like a "mound, eternally burnt, eternally scarred," suggesting that civilization is precarious and maintained only at torturous cost. And when Mr. Pepper, an old friend of Ridley Ambrose's from their undergraduate days at Cambridge, and also a passenger on the Euphrosyne, is described as being like a "fossilized fish," the reader is being prepared to take a long perspective of history. As later episodes depend on a sense of the antiquity and fragility of human enterprise, and still others on the ubiquity of death, these allusions form part of a large design, more and more intriguing as it grows in complexity.

The design incorporates all the concerns that reappear more fully developed in the later novels: the misunderstanding between parents and children; the inadequate preparation of women for life; male arrogance; the roles of man and woman in marriage; the nature of love, the male concept of the state as an intricate machine in which humans are simply replaceable parts; militarism as an instrument of the mechanical state, destroying both body and spirit; revulsion against the hypocrisy of organized religion; the incompetence of medical practitioners; how everything might be intelligible if one went back far enough; and art as a counterforce to the destructive power of impersonal nature.

A major part of the design is Rachel Vinrace, who is already on board waiting for her aunt and uncle, the Ambroses. Rachel is the daughter of a widower, raised by elderly maiden aunts in almost total seclusion from the world. At twenty-four she is at once a child, a woman, and a musician, her one accomplishment playing the piano. These aspects of her character gradually develop larger implications—as innocent abroad, as subservient woman in a man's world, and as artist. She will be dead of a tropical fever within six months, a period in which she reaches out for maturity and encounters the kinds of experience she has been protected from. Certainly the "voyage out" begins early to signify more than a pleasure cruise; it promises an "odyssey," emblematic of life. Thus readers of this novel are invited at the outset to participate in a search for meaning in the "profound and reasonless" contradictions that mold human existence.

At Lisbon, Mr. and Mrs. Richard Dalloway come aboard. Dalloway is a Member of Parliament, and, though a conservative, prides himself on being concerned about labor reforms and government in a theoretical, liberal way. The apparent warmth of his views and his rugged handsomeness are attractive to Rachel. Clarissa Dalloway is a sprightly conversationalist, rather superficial, but an acute observer of society. The Dalloways represent to Rachel the sophisticated world she has never known; conversations with them awaken in her questions about the relations between men and women and the whole of life; she wants Richard Dalloway "to tell her everything."

But Dalloway's description of the state as a highly complicated machine leaves Rachel dissatisfied. She feels that Dalloway is leaving out something important. Rachel wants from life a unity, a wholeness, that would reconcile all contradictions. Her unsophisticated thinking formulates for the first time the central preoccupation of all Woolf's fiction, the imagination's attempt to encompass time and process: ". . . if one went back far enough, everything was perhaps intelligible; everything was in common; for the mammoths who pastured in the fields of Richmond High Street had turned into paving stones and boxes full of ribbon, her aunts."

On the subject of love, Dalloway is more success-ful in swaying Rachel. Clarissa has prepared the way for him by confiding to Rachel that her husband is an ideal man who has given her everything. Moreover, Rachel knows that her ignorance of life is abysmal and that the experience of love might "unveil the stars." But her romantic euphoria is interrupted. One day on deck, Dalloway has just asked Rachel if she knows what "love" means, when a pair of warships appear in the distance. The vessels have the sinister appearance of gray, eyeless beasts seeking their prey.

This picture of ugliness and destruction, coming immediately after talk about "love," startles Rachel. The link suggested between love and death is hardly more than a shadow cast momentarily across Rachel's uneasy thoughts. The warships as symbols of death might seem to derive from Dalloway's description of the state as a great machine, and the linking of death with love only coincidental. But an unmistakable con-nection is made in the next sequence of events on board the Euphrosyne.

Flattered by the innocent admiration of Rachel, Dalloway one day on impulse passionately embraces her. That night in her sleep she has a terrifying vision. She dreams that she is walking down a long tunnel with slimy walls that opens into a vault, in which she finds herself trapped with a deformed man who like some hideous animal "squatted on the floor gibbering." The unsettling episode with Dalloway has stirred her long-

repressed instincts. All night long, voices seem to moan
for her, and she dreams that the ship is taken over by
barbarian men who snuffle at her locked door. For
Rachel it is a nightmare that, following the emotional
involvement with Dalloway, leaves her disturbed for
the rest of her short life. The immediate emotional
problem, however, is solved when the Dalloways leave
the ship at the next port of call.

When Rachel arrives at the resort hotel in San
Marino, her sexual impulses, now linked with death in
her own subconscious, are presented with new chal-
lenges in two men her own age, Terence Hewet and St.
John Hirst. They are both attractive, though intellectually arrogant. Hirst, who is going into the academic life
at Cambridge, asserts that he will become one of the
people who really matter. Hewet, who plans to be a
writer (though he has yet to finish his first novel)
admits that he is only second-rate—about like Thackeray.

Of the two, Rachel is more attracted to Hewet
because he combines in his character elements of both
male rationality and female intuition. In this respect he
is reminiscent of Richard Dalloway, described by his
wife as "man and woman as well." Rachel and Hewet
feel an alternation of attraction and repulsion as their
relationship develops. Rachel senses the possibility of
love between them but is unwilling to commit herself to
this mysterious condition while she knows so little
about everything.

Her attempts to expand her knowledge are both
comic and pathetic. She tries Gibbon's *Decline and
Fall of the Roman Empire,* contemporary fiction,
Burke's speech on Reconciliation with the American
Colonies, and poetry. But her principal mode is visual
and introspective. She observes the vistas of South

American mountains and forest from the mountaintop. She watches the busy ants. She explores the hotel and its rooms. In her delirium as she is dying, Rachel has the sense of being able to look through walls, to push back the perimeters of her physical world, to break through the nightmare vault that was her earlier vision of death.

The next-to-last stage in Rachel's exploration of life—the last being the delirious visions of her illness—is an expedition of six travelers upriver to visit a native village. During this ten-day trip, she and Hewet agree to be married, and the organism that she has picked up earlier from drinking water out of a stream begins its deadly work. The allusions that established the symbolic overtones of the voyage out from England are renewed.

It is described as a journey away from the articulateness and differences between men, a journey into the past. There are references to prehistoric forces, to the Elizabethan explorers who left their mark on this territory, and the adventurer of only ten years past whose bones they expect to see near his ruined hut. When Hewet reads aloud from a book about how love endures, his words are mocked by the wild laugh of a bird and a monkey's chuckle. The references to historical time and the ironic commentary of nature on human affairs point up the transience of life and set a mood that becomes darker as the expedition proceeds. The trip up the river through a tunnel of foliage to a native village resembles Rachel's nightmare vision of the tunnel with the narrowing brick walls leading to the chamber and its gibbering little old man. Even in her moment of happiness as she and Hewet confess their love, she hears as in a nightmare "the cruel churning of water" in the nearby river.

Romantic love appears to be the theme of this story until it becomes shadowed by visions of death, after which the role of ingenue develops toward a more general representation, that of any human exploring the enigma of his existence. On the expedition upriver, Rachel's sense of reality becomes increasingly disturbed as the fever takes hold. With the final hallucinatory visions before death, it can be seen in retrospect that Virginia Woolf has been proposing that life itself is a long terminal fever.

The embarkation scene in chapter one, so much like a scene in Hades with Charon transporting souls across the Styx, prepares us to read the allegory of Rachel's short voyage out. She is the explorer who, eagerly but in ignorance, seeks experience and knowledge in a wider world. Like other innocents abroad of literature, her special qualification for this role is the inexperience that allows her to look at the obvious with a fresh and curious eye.

The story might have ended with Rachel's death, picturing life as a "view of the skeleton." But in that event, with so little of the heroic in Rachel, there would have been no elevating effect of tragedy, only a sense of dissatisfaction with the inscrutable ways of fate. But in a final chapter—structurally a coda—a terrifying electrical storm is described and, as it passes, its restorative, energizing effect on the residents of the hotel. Though Rachel's flame has been snuffed out, the warm illumination of the general life burns on.

Virginia Woolf does not attempt to persuade either herself or the reader that such a view is finally comforting. She proffers a much more matter-of-fact idea: that life has infinite attractions of the "flesh"; that it is better to look at the flesh than at the skeleton underneath; and that the use of art is to produce a likeness of the flesh that will attractively conceal the skeleton without denying that it is there. The reader's "present moment" is expanded by the imagined possibilities, and he sees himself, his life, and the "whole of human life advancing nobly," as did Rachel's audience when she played Bach.

Rachel states the writer's problem bluntly to the would-be-writer Hewet: Why write? Music "says all there is to say at once." But that was a position Virginia Woolf herself could not accept. In her first novel and her second, *Night and Day*, she explored ways of transporting the reader into that "silent land" of subconscious perceptivity, which, though wordless, is a vital part of what the novelist produces.

Night and Day, her second novel, was published in 1919. It takes for its thesis woman's place in the worlds of society, intellect and marriage. Woolf begins with a narrative of exterior fact about women's subjection to men, but soon introduces the idea that dominates the conclusion of *The Voyage Out*, that there is a common life in which everyone participates.

This, we have seen, is not a wholly satisfactory solution to the problem of mortality from the viewpoint of the individual. Virginia Woolf tries in *Night and Day* to make a general life more acceptable by linking it with the unifying power of love, which would seem to be an attempt to explain one mystery by means of another. But *Night and Day* embodies one of mankind's most ancient insights into the nature of the relationship between man and woman: the concept of the universe as a system of two powerful forces interacting and complementary.

The design for this concept is a circle bisected by a sigmoid (S shape) that divides the circle into two areas of dark and light; in the dark area is a small disc of light, and in the light a small disc of dark. The Taoist *yin-yang* is implicit in the title and in the supporting imagery of light and dark throughout the novel. An approach to this concept is discernible in *The Voyage Out*, in which the view of sex as a combination of complementary qualities is apparent in Clarissa Dalloway's praise of her husband as "man and woman too" and in Rachel's preference for the intuitive-rational Hewet to the rational Hirst.

In the psychology of Woolf's view of sex, the female *yin* is characteristically intuitive and the male *yang* rational. *Night and Day* is essentially the account of two human natures striving to overcome the deceptive self-sufficiency of their individual selves to achieve a combination of forces representing true strength. Katharine and Denham in their search for ways to establish communication, discover love as a fundamental human necessity, whether in the sexual attraction of man and woman or universalized in philanthropy.

Katharine Hilbery, daughter of the editor of a law journal, is bored by the duties shared with her mother as curator of the household shrine of her famous grandfather, a poet, and distressed by her mother's disorganized attempts to write his biography. Ancestor worship in this upper-middle-class society means to Katharine male dominance out of the past.

Katharine is being persuaded by her mother to marry a young would-be poet, William Rodney. If she does, Katharine is aware that she will be submitting to the patriarchal family pattern, subordinating her life completely to that of her husband. Rodney is resentful whenever Katharine disagrees with him. To his chagrin, she prefers the Elgin marbles to Titian, gray days to sunny, and does not like apricots. He sees no reason why she should have opinions of her own. She knows

enough "for all decent purposes." He asks, "What do
you women want with learning?"

The answer to Rodney's question is found in the
life led by Mary Datchett. Daughter of a Lincolnshire
rector, she has left home and established a place of her
own in London. She works at increasing her knowledge
of literature and the arts, visits the British Museum
during her lunch hour, and sponsors meetings. She is
devoted to practical and theoretical matters, such as
land rents and voting rights, and has made an important role for herself in the women's suffrage movement.

In Mary Datchett, Woolf presents a woman who
has broken out of the female's traditional roles. Socially, she is without pretensions and free to entertain
the people she wants for her own reasons; intellectually, she is autonomous; and in marriage, she is free to
choose. Katharine, on the other hand, finds herself in
the traditional pattern: socially, an ornament of the
drawing room; intellectually, trained to be an admirer
of male accomplishment; and in marriage, expected to
run the household and serve as a looking-glass reflecting the male image at twice its size.

Both young women are acquainted with Ralph
Denham, a lawyer who wants to write books on socio-
logical subjects, publishing occasionally in the legal
journal edited by Katharine's father. Denham supports
his widowed mother and her large family in an ugly
house in Highgate. He feels just as trapped by his family situation as Katharine does by hers. Mary Datchett,
the liberated woman, is attracted to Denham and discovers that falling in love is not quite the rational process she had thought. At one point, she is ready to give
up everything in London and go with him to live in a
cottage in the country, where he will write his book on
English village life. It is Denham who points out that

such a course would bring her full circle to the domestic life she had so recently escaped. When Denham does propose marriage, she refuses—but only because she sees that he is really in love with Katharine.

As for Katharine, she continues to struggle with the family pressures constraining her to marry William Rodney. Without a clear course for her own life, she vacillates between breaking with him and accepting him as her husband. But this struggle only represents a deeper one—with the light and dark elements of her own nature: "This astonishing precipice, on the one side of which the soul was active and in broad daylight, on the other side of which it was contemplative and dark as night."

With this formulation of Katharine's problem, her self-conflict is shifted from the exterior, social to the interior, subjective, which is the arena of vital action in all Woolf's novels. And with this shift, the novel takes on a quality that is uniquely Virginia Woolf's. Katharine rejects her former view that romantic dreams (of a magnanimous, heroic lover) are the realities of the external world. But she has no means for facing the real world of ugliness and injustice without her dreams. When she confides to Denham that now she can't see much sense in having ideals, he provides her with means for connecting her inner world with the world around her, asking why she calls them "ideals"—why not call them "dreams"?

At this point Katharine perceives for the first time that her own "dreams" may have a valid connection with worthwhile activities in the real world. Acting on this new understanding, Katharine makes a start. She breaks with William Rodney and begins to concentrate on her study of mathematics and astronomy. She now works openly on the mathematics that for years she had concealed. She who had always been at everyone's beck and call during the day is now secluded, doing her own work.

In a primary sense then, the book's title refers to the night of Katharine's previous servitude to social convention and the day of her new freedom. Her previous existence of meaningless activity from which she escaped into romantic dreams has become a life of constructive possibilities, and the dream world is transformed into a potent source of motivation and energy.

But once Katharine has set her course, dark and light take on further meaning: they come to represent the nature of the relationship between man and woman, and the whole condition of human life in Woolf's version of the interaction of opposites. The apparent differences that are early revealed between Katharine and Denham really exist—they always find themselves in a state of tension together.

By himself, imagining an "interview" with Katharine, Denham jots down fragmentary ideas about their relationship. What he writes says in effect that woefully inadequate as communication is between two people, it is still the best we know; it gives each access to another world independent of oneself; and especially that world that two minds can create together—"a vision flung out in advance of actual circumstances." When words fail Denham, his pen begins to fill the blank spaces with "blots fringed with flames."

This doodle with its circling flames represents that "incalculable force" that Mary Datchett had observed in both Katharine and Denham. To Denham, they are emblematic of the universal energy participated in by individual beings. He expresses this view to Katharine, naming all their acquaintances, linking them together in a vision of an orderly world.

Woolf employs light and light effects richly throughout *Night and Day* to symbolize this energy and cohesiveness. In the final episode, the symbolism is worked out in great detail so as to illuminate in a literal sense the complexity of her themes. Lamps, lights, flames, starlight—all imply the incomprehensible system within which for a time the lives of Katharine and Denham were brought together: "she held in her hands for one brief moment the globe which we spend our lives in trying to shape, round, whole, and entire from the confusion of chaos."

Night and Day appears in summary, like *The Voyage Out*, to be the plodding affair of external incident that many of its early readers found it to be. But given its intended symbolic interaction of light and dark, it becomes a large, foggy gloom shot through with sudden fires and glowing lights. There are scenes of impressive power and others of moving sensitivity, when the external objective world persuasively dramatizes the inner world. More often, the juncture is only a mechanical one—the reader sees what is intended but is unmoved by it. By the time Virginia Woolf was ready to write her next novel, *Jacob's Room*, she had combined what she learned in writing *The Voyage Out* and *Night and Day* with her experiments in the short stories to produce her unique style.

◇◇

3

Short Stories

and

Jacob's Room

I like going from one lighted room to another,
such is my brain to me; lighted rooms;
and the walks in the fields are corridors. . . .

During the time she was writing *Night and Day*, Virginia Woolf experimented in short stories, vignettes, and sketches with a method that would relate events on the surface of life to events in the mind. An entry in the diary of 1920 preserves her conviction that three of these short pieces of fiction would make possible a "new form for a new novel." What she meant is not clear, and one must turn to the short stories for enlightenment.

In "Kew Gardens," first published in 1917, she attempts several apparently different things that when seen in their relationships give some idea of what she meant by "new form." Since she wanted to make the reader feel something that has nothing to do with the story, it is no surprise to find that there is no "story," only sets of people wandering through a park: a young married couple and their children, a young man in charge of an incompetent elderly man, two elderly women of the lower middle classes, and a girl and boy in love. Also "wandering" in the park is a snail, though it moves scarcely a leaf's width in the course of the narrative.

The snail has "nothing to do with the story" and consequently has most to do with the "new form." Taking the snail's point of view, Virginia Woolf provides a fresh perspective. She tries to regain "the microscopic eye" that mankind has lost—not for the sake of examining minute particles of earth, but for the sense of a slower time scale that the microscopic focus, with its intensification, provides. Time and its relativity, we discover, is that "something that has nothing to do with the story."

In "The Mark on the Wall," Virginia Woolf goes on from the concept that intensity of experience is the true measure of time, to insist that inner experience is the primary value. Novelists of the future, she predicts, will explore the depths of the inner experience, "leaving the descriptions of reality more and more out of their stories." In the nine pages of this sketch, she explores the depths. The "mark," in the end seen to be a snail, serves only as a point of contact with "reality," while the mind runs free in a process of association.

The third of the three short fictions, "An Unwritten Novel," is a preparatory sketch of a character for the kind of novel the new form would allow. It is Virginia Woolf's account of being in a railway compartment, constructing an imaginary life for the woman sitting opposite, a lonely unattached woman, Woolf surmises, making her annual visit to a married sister. The visit is described in elaborate detail—the lukewarm reception, the petty humiliations, and her romantic fixation on James Moggeridge, a commercial traveler—until the narrator (and the reader) believe in it. Then the woman gets off at a station where she is met by her son and the two walk away together quite happily.

We are persuaded of the actuality of "Minnie" and "Moggeridge" as the narrator builds their fictitious lives. We are also persuaded of the actuality of the woman in the train compartment. But as Woolf develops the imagined existence of an unattractive, lonely, dependent woman, we come to believe more and more in the reality that is imagined. Rather than being asked to suspend our disbelief, we are reminded from time to time that this is the "actual" Minnie and this the "other." Woolf tells us each time the two are brought together that both are "real," thus using real life to validate imaginary life.

Yet when the woman descends from the train and goes off with her son, the "Minnie" of the narrator's

imagination, the Minnie of "no love, life, faith, husband, children" is destroyed, and the writer's despair at
the loss of the creature of her imagination is under-
standable: "Well, my world's done for! What do I
stand on? What do I know? That's not Minnie. There
never was Moggeridge. Who am I? Life's bare as bone."

But this is not a defeat for the method. Her momentary cry of despair is followed by a resurgence of
the imagination that returns again and again to the real
world for nourishment: "And yet the last look of them
. . . floods me anew. Mysterious figures! Mother and
son. Who are you?" Her method, like that of Marianne
Moore, was to mine the outer world of "fact" to get the
raw material for creating imaginary gardens with real
toads in them.

In writing *Jacob's Room*, she gave the method its
first test in a long work of fiction. Half a century after
the publication of that novel in 1922, readers frequently overlook its innovative qualities and fall into
some critics' misconceptions about it—that the characters are not "definite" or "memorable," and that even
Jacob does not leave the reader with an impression of
his individuality. These misjudgments derive from
preconceptions about what novels in general should be
and what, therefore, Woolf was attempting to do in this
one. *Jacob's Room* is not a great novel, but it is innovative and finely wrought—her first success in bringing
together symbiotically the inner and outer worlds.

The story of Jacob Flanders from early in life to
his death as a young man, is narrated in a series of
episodes about his childhood, his years in Cambridge
University, his social and his antisocial inclinations, his
friendships with men, his connections with women, and
his journey to France and Greece. The early episodes
are variations on life and death—the light and dark of

existence—a thematic continuance of the preceding novel *Night and Day*.

One example illustrates the characteristic richness and subtlety of associations. As a young boy, Jacob begins to collect butterflies. Their names, including painted ladies and white admirals, associate the ephemeral life of butterflies with the ephemeral life of man. But Jacob finds the butterflies near some old Roman ruins, suggesting both mortality and persistence through succeeding generations.

Jacob's undergraduate days at Cambridge are depicted as a flickering of lights beginning to glow intensely as mind kindles mind. But there is a cautionary word about inspiration that is developed to thematic importance: when you speak of intellectual fervor, you mean not just Greek or Latin or a certain place like Cambridge, but a particular writer saying a particular thing, and the fever pitch when "mind prints upon mind indelibly." This kind of relationship is extended into the next phase of Jacob's life in London, where, reading Plato, he has the argument stowed away in his mind "and for five minutes Jacob's mind continues, alone, onwards into the darkness."

Jacob's room in London, with its rose and ram's skull carved in wood over the door, becomes the center of what we know about him, piece by disconnected piece. He reads a lot, both in his room and in the British Museum, and writes a few essays, which are returned to him by the journals. He takes a mistress, then another—Florinda, Fanny—women of passing consequence to him.

Bored with London, he goes to the continent. Jacob's letters to his friend Bonamy, whose own preference in writing was for the "definite, the concrete, and the rational," leave him puzzling over their

"dark sayings." These have to do with Jacob's catching
a glimpse of the world under the aspect of eternity,
countering the other tendency in himself to be content
in the life of the moment with friends and mistress. Up
to this time, in young manhood, Jacob has been happy
in his mastery of the flesh.

Now in Greece, on the site of ancient civilizations,
Jacob submits himself to the austere, self-obliterating
view of the skeleton beneath the flesh. He confronts the
human predicament described by Woolf in Words-
worthian images: as children, "we start transparent,"
and then behind our pane of glass "the cloud thick-
ens." Besieged by darkness, we can resist only by
maintaining a counterpressure from within. In this context, the story of Jacob Flanders is also the story of
Jacob's "room," and the rooms throughout that stand
for the mind—Jacob's mind, as represented by his
rooms in Cambridge and London, and Man's collective
mind, as represented by museum reading rooms—all
resisting the darkness pressing in.

The reading room reassures us that we belong to a
stream of existence, and by contributing to that stream
we share in its continuance—as Jacob shares in it at
Cambridge, receiving this "gift from the past." Feeling
"masterly," he looks out over the courtyard. A sense of
"old buildings and time" comes to him and he thinks of
himself as "the inheritor." This passage is only in part
an indulgent smile for Jacob's youthful confidence—it
also anticipates his role in the novel. What is this role,
since Jacob, despite his youth and "beauty" is in no
way extraordinary? What is the significance of his receiving a "gift from the past"? In what sense is he
"masterly," and how does he "inherit"?

These are questions which only the rich complexity of the whole novel can answer satisfactorily. But

some of the lines of association can be indicated, one of which depends on our seeing the implications of the names "Jacob" and "Flanders." In the biblical story, Jacob and Esau were born twins, Esau becoming a hunter, and Jacob (coming after, being second-born), a herdsman, representing two aspects of the developing Jewish people.

Virginia Woolf gave both aspects in Jacob Flanders's character: he combines the "hairy" man, Esau (discernible in the "wild horse" discovered in himself in Greece) and the "smooth" man, Jacob (who could take Plato's argument for five minutes on into the darkness). Given this context, intellect is in the ascendancy, and the name Jacob stands for higher possibilities of civilization: learning, art, the "light" of Cambridge. His surname, Flanders, takes its import from the undertones of war that sound through the last third of the novel. As Flanders, like the battlefields in Flanders during 1914–18, where he is killed, Jacob falls to the darkness of human history. In this doubleness, the novel shows Jacob both as inheritor and as victim—the riches and potentiality of the human enterprise are his, but also its tendencies to self-destruction.

In *The Voyage Out* and *Night and Day*, Virginia Woolf had described the confrontation between two approaches to life—one intuitive, valuing personal relationships; the other analytical, coveting power, and zealous to control events. In *Jacob's Room*, she makes the contrast more explicit by personifying these forces. The fact-hunters, the power-seekers, are ministers of government, manipulators of finance. Representing the other side are the novelists, whom the "men in clubs and Cabinets" refer to when they say that "character-drawing is a frivolous fireside art."

Woolf completes her summary of the charge

against novelists made by the power-seekers: "They say novelists never catch [the unseizable force]; that it goes hurtling through their nets and leaves them torn to ribbons." In this way, she connects what she is saying in the novel about life with what she wants to say about writing, which for her is the "process" of discovering life put down in words.

Jacob's Room is more directly about writing itself than either of the two preceding novels, in its assertions that language and writing are integral to the process of discovering. Virginia Woolf bases her position on the Dostoyevsky statement, remembered by Katharine Hilbery in *Night and Day*: "It's life that matters, nothing but life—the process of discovering—the everlasting and perpetual process, not the discovery itself at all." It is a position for which fiction is peculiarly suitable. For in fiction the reader discovers from scene to scene what the life of that fiction is—he participates in a process in which life is revealed.

A chapter at the center of the novel focuses on writing's part in the "process." Mrs. Flanders, in her letters to Jacob in London "can never, never say, whatever it may be—probably this—Don't go with bad women, do be a good boy; wear your thick shirts, and come back, come back, come back to me. But she said nothing of the kind." Her letters are, in fact, full of local gossip. In her letters (as in all our letters, Woolf implies) "the hand . . . is scarcely perceptible, let alone the voice or the scowl."

Even the masters of language have turned to letters in hopes of "reaching, touching, penetrating the individual heart"—and failed. This admission seems to imply that even writing cannot offer much help in deciphering the mystery of our lives or capturing its indescribable agitation. Yet words are all we have—unless we capitulate to the "wild horse" in us, which is word-less.

Jacob's room, throughout the novel, resembles a mind that objectifies what it knows in verbal forms—forms that are intended to withstand the ravages of time. Woolf observes about someone buried on the moor, "Tom Gage cries aloud so long as his tombstone endures." In this sense, Jacob's rooms, which manifest his own vital nature, constitute the living monument devised by Virginia Woolf to perpetuate the memory of Jacob.

But Woolf does more in this ancient prescription against oblivion than take comfort in monuments. She faces honestly the challenge to herself as a writer to create something that will endure. The extent of her ambitions may be seen from comparing an entry in her diary, to the effect that she made up *Jacob's Room* while looking into the fire at Hogarth House, with her description of the anonymous man in Soho, which comes at the end of the "lamps of London" section:

The little man . . . must have squatted before the fire in innumerable lodging houses, and heard and seen and known so much that it seems to utter itself volubly from dark eyes, loose lips . . . his face sad as a poet's, and never a song sung.

Just before this section appears the comment, "For my own part, I find it exceedingly difficult to interpret songs without words," which implies the magnitude of the task she set herself in this and all her subsequent novels: to give words to the song of the anonymous man, and to the wordless songs of Betty Flanders, Florinda and Fanny, and Jacob. The song of Jacob has words, and words stay in the mind. They stay because a particular author, Virginia Woolf, is saying a particular thing at fever pitch. When that occurs, "mind prints upon mind indelibly." This analysis of the writer's creative act marks *Jacob's Room* as the transition to Woolf's art of fiction.

In form and style it is different from the preceding novels. Those that come after it, though strongly individual, are in the main based on the experimental writing in *Jacob's Room*. Can it be said then that the three short stories ("Kew Gardens"; "The Mark on the Wall"; "An Unwritten Novel") provide a "program" for the novels? That question can be answered briefly by indicating how the material of *Jacob's Room* is programmed according to the innovations in the stories.

The first is alternation of focus to intensify experience. This is accomplished by expanding and contracting the chronological frame of reference: (1) Roman settlement in Britain, the remains of Roman forts in modern times, Betty Flanders's brooch and needles lost among the ruins, the butterflies' fleeting existence above them; (2) the derivation of Jacob's name from the brotherhood of Jacob and Esau, the representation of both elements in the quarter-century span of his life, and the centaurlike version of Jacob-Esau in his inner life (the "wild horse" joined with intellectual aspiration); (3) the flickering light of civilization down through the ages, the glow of intellectual activity over Cambridge, the illumination from the reading room in the British Museum, Jacob's room, where he reads Plato—the varieties of changing focus from distant to near can only be suggested.

The second innovation was aimed at establishing the primacy of inner experience. This is accomplished by assessing the value of all external events according to the inner response. Woolf's metaphors point consistently within, thus: "all history backs our pane of

glass," "mind prints upon mind indelibly," and the repeated sequence of images leading from civilization to
room to mind. The primacy of inner experience is most
satisfyingly demonstrated by the whole novel, which
brings every movement toward a restingplace in the
mind of the reader, where Jacob is brought back to life
by the final sentence.

That sentence ("She held out a pair of Jacob's old
shoes") also indicates the third area of Woolf's ex-
perimentation, which was to make concretely vivid the
relationship between the real world and the world of
the imagination. She believed in the imagination and
distrusted the "cheapness" of reality. Yet she almost
rejected the "silent land" of inner perception: how
could one interpret songs without words? *Jacob's Room*
was her first substantial attempt to enter the "silent
land" and return with its song in communicable form.

4

Mrs. Dalloway

Do not cut down trees.
Universal love:
the meaning of the world.

In her next novel, *Mrs. Dalloway*, she continues to work out her problems of theme and form along the lines laid out first in the short stories and *Jacob's Room*. Thus most of the "ideas" in *Mrs. Dalloway* are carried over from *Jacob's Room*, though she adds the major theme of insanity. But that is also simply a development of two ideas in the preceding novel: (1) that there must be a positive (loving) connection between the inner and outer life; and (2) that institutional power is the expression of a negative (unloving) connection, Jacob's death being attributed to war, a manifestation of institutional mania for power over individuals.

Millions of Jacobs died in 1914–18, Woolf insists, because of this mania in high places. Now, in *Mrs. Dalloway*, Virginia Woolf shows us another victim—Septimus Warren Smith, who is clinically insane as a result of four years in combat. Smith falls into the hands of two medical practitioners whose energies are directed toward dominating their patient instead of healing him.

Clarissa Dalloway, too, is passing through a mental crisis, precipitated partly by a recent severe illness. During the single day in which the events of *Mrs. Dalloway* take place, the stories of these two—Clarissa and Septimus—are intertwined, though they never meet. Clarissa moves away from isolation toward an acceptance of life in all its puzzling complexity; Septimus moves ever deeper into isolation and finally suicide.

The narrative present of *Mrs. Dalloway* spans most of a bright, warm June day in London some five years after the war of 1914–18. But the tunneling into the past (Virginia Woolf's expression) goes back for thirty years. Readers familiar with *The Voyage Out*, in which the Dalloways appear briefly, will find no mention of that part of their past in this novel. All events, both past and present, build toward Clarissa's dinner party, when they are brought together in new relationships. The following summarizes briefly the major characters and action leading up to the party.

Mrs. Dalloway leaves her house in Westminster to buy flowers. On the way, she meets an old acquaintance, Hugh Whitbread, a functionary in the royal household. Later she observes a royal car passing through the streets and an airplane skywriting. Septimus Smith, a man in his early twenties, is seated on a bench in Regent's Park with his Italian wife Lucrezia (Rezia). He has spent four years in the war and is now mentally ill. He sees the skywriting and thinks that "they" are trying to get messages to him from the dead. Dr. Holmes, a general practitioner, has advised Mrs. Smith to get her husband interested in "real" things. But they are now on their way to see a specialist, Sir William Bradshaw.

Peter Walsh, in love with Clarissa thirty years ago, leaves the Dalloway house, where he has talked to Clarissa for the first time in many years, and walks toward Regent's Park. He follows a woman, out of sexual fantasy, until she disappears into a house. In the park, he naps, sitting on a bench. Leaving the park, he passes Septimus and Rezia and outside encounters a street singer, an old woman, singing a love song.

Richard Dalloway, Clarissa's husband, Member of Parliament, is at Lady Bruton's for lunch. She is a prominent society hostess who likes being involved with government affairs and moving masses of people around in various projects of her invention. Hugh

Whitbread, Clarissa's old friend, is also a guest. Lady Bruton wants these two men, both involved in government, to help her with one of her projects.

Septimus and Lucrezia keep their appointment with Sir William, who sees that the case is serious and advises Lucrezia to place her husband in a sanatorium. By now, Septimus identifies both doctors as his special persecutors. Both are, in fact, more interested in exercising power than in treating individuals.

Elizabeth Dalloway, Clarissa's daughter, about eighteen, leaves the Dalloway house for an afternoon with Miss Kilman, a woman of extraordinary unattractiveness. She is a religious zealot and has been proselytizing Elizabeth. Clarissa also fears that there is an unhealthy sexual relationship developing between the two. But as they take tea, Miss Kilman loses her hold on the girl. Elizabeth leaves the tea shop alone, boards a bus, and rides through London on a kind of voyage of independence, from which she returns "calm and competent."

Septimus and Rezia are in their sitting room. She is making hats, he going through the notes he has made of messages from the dead: "do not cut down trees; Universal love; the meaning of the world." Dr. Holmes chooses this moment to call—Dr. Holmes who "seemed to stand for something horrible to him. 'Human nature' he called him." As Holmes forces his way past Rezia into the room, Septimus leaps to his death. The novel concludes with the long section about the Dalloway party that evening, with the horror of Septimus's death offset by Clarissa's renewed vitality.

As Clarissa goes through the hours before her dinner party, she is besieged by memories of the past— stirring up doubts about her marriage to a man caught up in the endless round of politics; doubts about her daughter; and, most of all, doubts about herself. For she has just recovered from an illness, and to walk out into the bright June day is for her like the beginning of a new life—except for memories and the demands of the future that lie heavy upon her.

What she remembers is "scene after scene at Bourton," the country house where she grew to womanhood. Thirty years ago at Bourton, Clarissa and Peter Walsh had been much together. Clarissa came to feel that Peter's insistence on sharing everything, and his critical assessments, were finally intolerable, and she broke off their relationship. Yet there had been something vital between them, and in the years afterward Clarissa would never be certain she did not still love him.

Clarissa was also drawn to the energetic, attractive Sally Seton, who had shocked old Mrs. Parry at Bourton by running naked down the hall to the bathroom. Clarissa's memories of Sally are still, after thirty years, full and rich—how Sally had given her a flower and kissed her on the mouth just before Peter came upon them at the fountain one evening. The emotionally charged involvements with Peter and Sally were factors in Clarissa's decision to marry the steadier Richard Dalloway. And this decision, too, she believes thirty years later, had been a wise one. Peter would have destroyed her with his constant intrusions and critical remarks; and Sally would have dominated her.

These were Clarissa's memories as she went about preparing for her party that night, not just of events and relationships, but also a recollection of the atmosphere in which they occurred: the excited conversations, the laughter, the intuitive awareness of cross-purposes. These had been signs of life intensely felt, and she remembers how intense they had been.

But memory is inferior to present experience. What Clarissa loves now, she is certain, is before her eyes in the bright June morning: trees, and mothers with babies, the activity in nearby streets, the park itself appearing to lift its leaves "brilliantly, on waves of divine vitality." Clarissa sees this creative energy flowing from nature and shaping the present moment, the vital force of which is frequently symbolized by trees.

But the most attractive aspect of vitality appears in humans going about their business and their play— the "conduct of daily life" described in *Jacob's Room* as better than "the pageant of armies drawn out in battle array." A vision similar to that observed by Jacob, and identical in meaning, is experienced by Elizabeth when she cuts loose from Miss Kilman and in her excitement sets out to explore the city. She likes the uproar of the streets; she seems to hear the blare of trumpets, as if the crowds are marching to military music. The noise of the people in the streets is a "voice, pouring endlessly." This would carry them along. There is a Dickensian delight in movement and sounds in the description of Elizabeth's recommitment to life on her own, echoed by what Peter Walsh encounters on the warm June evening as he walks toward Clarissa's house—people opening doors, entering motor cars, rushing along the streets.

Despite these manifestations of human energy in masses, Woolf establishes the vital quality of life most strikingly in two solitary old women—one the street singer heard by Peter Walsh, the other the occupant of a room across the way from Clarissa's house. The old street singer's song at first is hardly intelligible; certainly she is no picture of vitality—nearly blind, and in rags. Her song, however, celebrates the invincible power of love, how love had lasted a million years, bubbling up like an ancient spring spouting from the earth, greening things, fertilizing.

Still remembering how once in some primeval May she had walked with her lover, this rusty pump, this battered old woman . . . would still be there in ten million years . . . the passing generations—the pavement was crowded with bustling middle class people—vanished like leaves, to be trodden under, to be soaked and steeped and made mould of by that eternal spring.

The whole passage about the street singer is one of those Woolf developed more through the devices of poetry than of prose. Its effect depends on the persuasiveness of the imagery to transform the reader's feeling for the old woman, whether pity or revulsion, into wonder and admiration. A tree without leaves, she is still an instrument from which the wind of creative energy elicits a song: "Cheerfully, almost gaily, the invincible thread of sound wound up into the air, like the smoke from a cottage chimney." It is an evocative piece of writing, persuasive indeed—but not convincing. The metaphors of the rusty pump and the cottage are obtrusive. The reader sees what they are meant to do and feels the poetry of them, but with reservation.

The second incident involving an old woman occurs in the course of the party at Dalloway's house. In developing the significance of this scene, Woolf employs a more successful technique. She does not attempt to move the reader by poetic statement to believe that the old woman represents life without despair. The scene is depicted in a matter-of-fact way. As Clarissa watches an old woman in her room across the street preparing for bed, there are none of the verbal associations with love, as in the street singer's song, to make their frank appeal to the reader's emotions. Yet the significance of what Clarissa sees, though tentative even in her mind, is sufficient to offset the despair that has been rising in her.

This episode occurs after Clarissa hears at the party about the young man (Septimus) who has killed himself. Thinking about his suicide, Clarissa feels that the disaster, the disgrace of Septimus, is hers. Guilt floods her: "She had schemed; she had pilfered." But, thinking that she doesn't deserve to be happy, nevertheless she is. Now she rejects the triumphs of youth, and has committed herself wholly to the process of living— "creating it every moment afresh."

On a previous occasion, when Clarissa had been sorting out her thoughts about the religious zealot Miss Kilman, she had seen the old woman climb the stairs to her room, alone, as if self-contained in her life. To Clarissa there had been something solemn in it. But with Miss Kilman and Peter Walsh on her mind—those two proselytizers of "religion" and "love"—she had thought of the old woman in connection with that kind of love and religion that can destroy the privacy of the soul the old woman seemed to have. The "supreme mystery" was this: "here was one room; there was another. Did religion solve that, or love?"

Now at the party, as she watches the old woman again, seeing her move around, Clarissa is fascinated. Several things are coming together in Clarissa's mind— the idea of the privacy of the soul, and the mystery of the separation of human lives; these things joining with her awareness of the activities, the laughing and shouting, going on all around her at the party. Suddenly no longer in despair, she no longer pities herself, nor the young man who had killed himself. As the old lady's light goes out, Clarissa thinks of that whole house, dark now, with all this activity going on around it. Putting out the light was like dying. It did not stop the activity of living; the pageant of life went on.

Clarissa takes comfort in this train of thoughts because of her "theory," confided to Peter Walsh in the old days. They had been riding up Shaftesbury Avenue in a bus when she felt herself everywhere—not "here, here, here," she said, tapping the back of the seat, "but everywhere." Her comfort in the relationship that she felt between the old woman across the way and the young man who killed himself derives from that part of her theory about the affinities between people and how one must seek out those who complete one: the "unseen part of us" might survive, "be recovered somehow attached to this person or that."

The line from Shakespeare, "Fear no more the heat of the sun," appearing several times, explains Clarissa's cryptic remark about the young man's suicide: "She felt glad that he had done it; thrown it away." One need not fear the disasters of the physical life. Clarissa feels that if the young man had thrown his life away, she has caught it in hers. If the young man could complete his life in hers, then Clarissa could complete her life in others. It was a mystery—"here was one room; there was another"—but no longer a despairing mystery. This quality of excitement bubbling up from new-born vitality is what Peter Walsh recognizes in Clarissa at the book's conclusion: "What is it that fills me with extraordinary excitement? It is Clarissa, he said."

Virginia Woolf celebrated this ongoing vitality in many ways in her novels—welling up in love, at parties, and in the ordinary business of everyday life.

She placed it in opposition to the mania of those in positions of power to control the course of events. In *Jacob's Room*, these were the men in clubs and cabinets. In *Mrs. Dalloway*, signs of power are everywhere: the royal coat of arms emblazoned on Hugh Whitbread's dispatch case; the automobile and a face "of the very greatest importance" glimpsed against its dove-gray interior; the ceremonial marching of troops; and the prime minister himself at the Dalloways' party.

Accompanying these symbols and panoply of institutional power, there is the pervasive sense of the damage done to human lives by the individual wielders of power: the waste of Hugh Whitbread's genuine qualities in the servilities of his position as a court functionary; the persistent meddling of Lady Bruton, utilizing her position in society to move people around as if they were pieces in a little game of her own. When Lady Bruton naps, we are informed, her arm assumes the position of a field marshal's holding his baton.

This malicious observation springs out of Woolf's indignation, but one of the measures of her skill as a novelist is the ability to discipline strong feelings into the lasting instrument of art: for instance, the subtle paralleling of the dove-gray car of Sir William Bradshaw to the royal car. Sir William, the psychiatrist who takes over Septimus Smith from Dr. Holmes, is another manifestation of the established order as malevolent. His sinister compulsion to dominate those who come within his control is linked through the case of Septimus to the political powers in Whitehall: it is "they" who provided the shambles of war in which his sanity was damaged, and it is Sir William who completes the job.

We are never allowed to forget the war: the painful picture of Lady Bexborough opening a bazaar with the message in hand of her son's death in combat; the company of soldiers marching to a cenotaph; and through it all the presence of Septimus Smith, a shambling, broken figure, who signals institutional guilt whenever he appears.

Virginia Woolf exposes relentlessly the mania to dominate of people like Lady Bruton, Sir William, and Dr. Holmes. The clinical madness of Septimus is represented as a consequence in their manipulations—indirectly, as in the case of Lady Bruton's political and social schemes, and directly in the perverted "healing" of Bradshaw and Holmes.

Septimus is the victim of a war-induced neurosis. Having volunteered early in the war of 1914–18, he suffered for four years the frustration of his idealistic impulse to "save England for Shakespeare." Withstanding the successive traumas of combat, he is stricken by the survivor's guilt after his friend Evans is killed. Crippled within, he seeks out Lucrezia to marry her, with the instinctive knowledge that her health is what his sickness needs. She appears to him as the tree of life,

as if all her petals were about her. She was a flowering tree; and through her branches looked out the face of a lawgiver, who had reached a sanctuary where she feared no one.

His instinct was right and she is good for him, but because she is inexperienced and a foreigner, she is not capable of protecting him against the malpractices, condoned by society, of such "healers" as Holmes and Sir William.

Sir William, a large distinguished-looking man,

would not appear to be insane in any clinical sense. But he makes everyone profoundly uneasy in his presence. He is a self-made man, we discover, who has permitted himself to be shaped by the materialistic values that reward domination. In treating his patients he invoked all the forces of society to gain their submission. "Naked, defenceless, the exhausted, the friendless received the impress of Sir William's will. He swooped; he devoured. He shut people up." In his compulsion to put people away, Woolf casts Sir William as an agent of death. For insanity, as she describes it, is isolation from people, from things, from all the stuff of life—death, in short.

Sanity she identifies with life—the physical substance of it—women nursing babies, the blare of trumpets, legs moving energetically down the street. Even Richard Dalloway holding Clarissa's hand, though not the passionate moment of the kind he had imagined when he resolved to say I love you, is a moment of shared physical intimacy—it lives.

Peter Walsh, on the contrary, creating lurid fantasies around the woman he follows through the streets, is to a degree insane, to a degree dead, in that what he submits himself to is isolation: "All this one could never share—it smashed to atoms." The emptiness of Walsh's fantasy is like that of Katharine Hilbery's dream in *Night and Day*—her "magnanimous hero" riding his horse by the sea—a waste of imaginative power.

Walsh is torn between wanting to share and wanting to isolate himself. His life had been a constant vacillation, chasing one woman, then another, interspersed with "work, work, work." So that when in the end he is strongly moved by the vitality of Clarissa, it is not certain that this commitment is anything more than physical attraction or more than momentary. What is certain is that Clarissa has come through her own struggle against self-isolation and confirmed her rebirth into the health of shared existence.

In giving the "world of the sane and the insane side by side" (her primary objective in this novel), Virginia Woolf shows the sane reaching out to life—like Clarissa, recognizing in the old woman across the street someone whose life touches hers. Though her treatment of this idea is lyric, she does not attempt to screen the unpleasant or tragic with lyricism. Death is the dissonance that keeps her song complex and intriguing. In Clarissa, for instance, there is double awareness of mortality—through her recent serious illness and through having witnessed in girlhood the death of her gifted sister, crushed by a falling tree. The tree, so often in Woolf's writing the image of persistent life, by this accident reinforces the ambiguity of existence—like the light of *Night and Day*, it contains a portion of its opposite.

Many circumstances in *Mrs. Dalloway*, including the terrifying medical experience of Septimus Smith, were drawn from Virginia Woolf's life. The original intention to have Clarissa kill herself—in the pattern of Woolf's own intermittent despair—was rejected in favor of a "dark double" who would take that act upon himself. Creating Septimus Smith led directly to Clarissa's mystical theory of vicarious death and shared existence, saving the novel from a damaging imbalance on the side of darkness. Virginia Woolf's success in using her own madness as a subject for fiction, evidently provided the necessary confidence for attempting the equally delicate naterials of her next novel, *To the Lighthouse*, which concerned her unhappy childhood and the memories, still sensitive, of her parents.

5

◇◇◇

To the Lighthouse

And life, what was that?
It was only a light passing
over the surface and vanishing,
as in time she would vanish.

In her diary Virginia Woolf wrote that she wanted to present the personalities of her father and mother in *To the Lighthouse*, and St. Ives (where they spent their summers) and childhood. Aware that involvement with material so close to her own life could produce a damaging tone of nostalgia and regret, she avoided these with great technical skill, employing several points of view to minimize any overpowering emotional fixation and introducing comic aspects of domestic life to further reduce sentimentality. But what lifts this novel above the level of the ordinary family chronicle is Woolf's treatment of the human condition in an inscrutable universe. The multiple perspectives and the variations of tone serve chiefly to integrate episode, scene, and character toward this end, which is an intricately articulated response to the question "What is life?"

To the Lighthouse takes place in the Ramsay summer home on an island off the coast of Scotland. The surrounding sea, the beach, the receding sand dunes, a fishing village—these comprise a world small enough to show all its elements interacting, and sufficiently isolated to heighten symbolic implications.

The house itself is more suggested than described—an unremarkable three stories and attic. At a distance, beyond the bay, is the lighthouse. It conveys the impression of something that is part of this world, yet in some way beyond it, which is how the Ramsays see it—both as a fact in a real world and something metaphysical, or even personal, as when Mrs. Ramsay identifies herself with "the long stroke" of the beacon.

This thematic relationship is developed throughout the novel, from "The Window" (everything focuses on Mrs. Ramsay), through "Time Passes" (Mrs. Ramsay dies), to "The Lighthouse," in which her family and friends go on without her, but seeing the world now through her. At the beginning of part one, Mrs. Ramsay sits in the drawingroom window knitting a pair of stockings and overseeing her six-year-old son James as he cuts pictures from a catalogue. She has just assured him that if the weather is fine he can go to the Lighthouse the next day. Mr. Ramsay, who has been walking on the terrace, overhears this promise, and stops at the window to say abruptly that James cannot go because it will rain tomorrow.

With Mr. Ramsay is Charles Tansley, his admiring young student of philosophy. They are discussing men, books, and ideas. When Tansley goes off to work on his thesis, Mr. Ramsay strides nervously up and down, contemplating what he believes to be the failure of his professional life, especially his writing about philosophy. He begins to dramatize his emotional state by reciting lines from "The Charge of the Light Brigade."

At a further remove from the house is Lily Briscoe, in her middle thirties, a painter, standing at her easel. Nearby is William Bankes, a widower, who watches Lily at work and asks questions about her painting, much to her discomfort. At a distance, among the elm trees, young Jasper Ramsay is shooting at starlings with his air rifle. Minta Doyle, a family friend, and Paul Rayley, her suitor, go walking on the beach with two of the Ramsay children, Nancy and Andrew. During this walk, Minta and Paul become engaged to be married. Meanwhile, after hearing his mother read the fairy tale of "The Fisherman and His Wife," James is sent off to bed, downcast in the certainty that he will not go to the Lighthouse the next morning.

Thus the opening scene establishes the little universe of this novel, with Mrs. Ramsay sitting in a window at its center. It should be noted, however, that her son James is with her at this center. For James, despite his resentment of Mr. Ramsay, will grow up to acquire that definite, dogmatic hardness that is his father's masculine quality, as he begins to realize, in part three, on the way to the Lighthouse.

Dinner is served. It is a special occasion. Minta and Paul are present, Lily Briscoe, the poet Augustus Carmichael, Charles Tansley, and William Bankes, for whose pleasure Mrs. Ramsay has had prepared a *boeuf en daube*. The dish is a success, and with the lighting of the candles and pouring of wine, conversation becomes lively. Lily, thinking about her painting, arranges a salt cellar on the cloth to remind herself of where to place a tree in the composition.

After dinner, Mrs. Ramsay goes upstairs to the bedroom of Cam and James to find them, at eleven o'clock, still awake. Cam is frightened by the pig skull hanging on the wall, but James will not permit it to be removed. Mrs. Ramsay covers the skull with her green shawl and leaves the children pacified. She joins her husband, who is reading a novel of Sir Walter Scott's. She knits a while and then picks up a book of poetry. Ramsay has finished his chapter in the Scott novel. It moves him deeply—partly because, still worrying about his professional achievement, he thinks that since Scott's work can retain its power in spite of time's erosion, perhaps his own will too. Mrs. Ramsay, seeing that her husband has stopped reading, puts down her own book. Standing at the window, she assures her husband, managing at once to restore his self-esteem and to convey her love for him, that he was right about tomorrow, it will be wet.

Part two, "Time Passes," begins with the house

being darkened for the night. "Night, however, succeeds to night." And with that transition, the novel moves from a temporal mode in which time is intensified and expanded through detailed revelation of states of mind, into a mode in which events are regarded coolly through external observation, and time thus compressed. Ten years pass, during which Mrs. Ramsay is said to die very suddenly; the war of 1914–18 begins, and Andrew, the older son, is killed in battle; Prue, the older daughter, dies in childbirth.

Mrs. McNab, the cleaning woman, lets the house go to the inroads of wind, sand, spiders, damp, and birds, until she receives sudden notice to have the house ready for occupancy. What is left of the Ramsay family—notably Mr. Ramsay, Cam, and James, though the other children Nancy and Jasper are also present—return and are joined by Lily Briscoe and Augustus Carmichael, who is now a poet of some reputation. The world of the Ramsays prepares to accommodate to a new generation in which Mrs. Ramsay, though dead, continues to be an influence.

In part three, "The Lighthouse," the lighthouse itself is a constant reminder of Mrs. Ramsay, who had felt an affinity with it. As Lily Briscoe thinks about Mrs. Ramsay, she takes up her painting of ten years back and seeks to complete her vision. Her meditation is articulated by a series of questions, with "what is life?" at the center. Like Mr. Ramsay, she thinks of individual existence as something inexplicable, maintaining itself precariously against a steadily encroaching chaos. But her outlook, unlike Mr. Ramsay's, which is abstract, is concretely visual. Now, ten years after she arranged the salt cellar on the tablecloth to remind herself of where to place a tree in her painting, she remembers and takes up the quest in her art.

James, Cam, and their father set out early one morning by boat, arriving at the Lighthouse by midday.

The deaths of Mrs. Ramsay, Andrew, and Prue, linked to deaths in Virginia Woolf's own life—her mother, brother Thoby, and stepsister Stella—might easily have produced the sentimentality that she feared. She was able to avoid it partly through reporting these events with strict economy. But she also implied their incidental nature in the vast sweep of time by enclosing the "reports" in brackets. In the case of Mrs. Ramsay, the "notation" of her death is subordinated even within the bracketed sentence:

[Mr. Ramsay, stumbling along a passage one dark morning, stretched his arms out, but Mrs. Ramsay having died rather suddenly the night before, his arms though stretched out, remained empty.]

And functionally, this passage has as much to do with the self-dramatizing aspect of Mr. Ramsay's character as it does with his wife's death.

The daughter Prue's death is provided with aesthetic distance by being placed in the narrative equivalent of a three-panel pictorial treatment—a triptych. The first and third panels of the triptych are in brackets. The first depicts her marriage:

[Prue Ramsay, leaning on her father's arm, was given in marriage. What, people said, could have been more fitting? And, they added, how beautiful she looked!]

The center panel consists of a paragraph in which the beautiful long evenings of late spring are described, along with the "strange intimation . . . that good triumphs, happiness prevails, order rules." The third panel, bracketed like the first, then reports Prue's death:

[Prue Ramsay died that summer in some illness connected with childbirth, which was indeed a tragedy, people said, everything, they said, had promised so well.]

The juxtaposition of these three scenes—Prue's beauty, the hopeful intimations of spring, and the idle chatter about Prue's death—arranged in a triptych, lends its ironic statement a formal detachment. Woolf enlarges that irony in the treatment of Andrew Ramsay's death that immediately follows.

It is reported in brackets, after which occurs an observation about the "usual tokens of divine bounty" in sea and sky disturbed by a warship and the oil slick of a sunken submarine. These ugly intrusions made it difficult to maintain the "sublime reflections" and "comfortable conclusions" that the beauties of sky and sea appeared to offer. A bracketed passage then reports what people said about their interest in poetry—how war had revived it. The pervasive irony of this section dealing with the deaths of Prue and Andrew can hardly be conveyed by synopsis. Virginia Woolf developed this portion of the novel by means of brackets to distance emotional events, the formal arrangement of a triptych, and ironic ambiguity. The resulting detachment, and the implication of cosmic disinterest in human affairs, darkens the novel.

But it would have been darker had she not included touches of comedy throughout. Mrs. McNab, in part two, is a notable example. She is the cleaning woman who looks after the house during the Ramsays' absences. Her droll grumblings, sloth, and (stereotyped) outlook of the menial make a pleasurable contrast with the poetic texture and elegiac mood that characterize most of "Time Passes." Woolf also humanizes such figures as Mrs. Ramsay, the managerial but self-sacrificing mother, and Mr. Carmichael, the sage and self-sufficient man, by causing us to smile at them occasionally, thus reducing their symbolic stiffness.

The comedy indeed does more than lighten tone —as, for example, in Mr. Ramsay's absurd behavior, charging up and down the terrace, gazing into the distance and throwing his arms about, as he imaginatively participates in the charge of the Light Brigade. Having established the comic aspects of Mr. Ramsay in part one, Woolf confers dignity and leadership upon him in part three without falsifying his essential contradictions and without letting him appear grandiose. In part three, aware of his posturing, we nevertheless recognize him as admirably human in the single-mindedness and courage he brings to his struggle against the forces of chaos—and these qualities are assessed not by us but by Lily Briscoe and his own rebellious son James, both reluctant witnesses. Through comic relief, Woolf lightened the pessimism without minimizing the serious engagement of the characters with their human predicament.

The Ramsays and their friends have many ways to combat the inimical powers surrounding them, through art, through intellect—and through the circle of affection and its "community of feeling," which was Mrs. Ramsay's way. Not everybody thought of her, however, as all sweetness and light. Mr. Carmichael, for example, detected in her an inclination to manage people. She sometimes doubts herself. Reading Grimm's fairy tale of the Fisherman's Wife, Mrs. Ramsay's thoughts turn to what people say about her —that she runs people's lives, that she is a matchmaker. The fairy tale produces a caricature of herself in her own mind, which through its patent overstatement of Mrs. Ramsay's faults, moves the reader to redress the balance of his own mind in her favor.

The story tells of a fisherman and his wife who live in a pigsty by the sea. When the flounder he catches one day reveals itself as an enchanted prince, the man's wife makes him exact money and position from the flounder. One exaction leads to another, and each time the fisherman returns to the flounder, the sea is more stormy and disturbed. The greedy, domineering wife, not content as king and emperor, finally becomes pope. When at last she wishes to be god, there is a terrible storm, during which the couple suddenly find themselves returned to their pigsty. "And there they are living still at this very time," concludes Mrs. Ramsay.

The parts of the story read to James by Mrs. Ramsay are interspersed with her various thoughts and those of Lily Briscoe, stretching over thirty-three pages of text. She thinks about her husband as she observes him, like the fisherman, looking out over the sea. Despite the implications of the pig's skull hanging on the bedroom wall, Mrs. Ramsay is not greedy for advancement like the fisherman's wife, and her managerial bent is almost wholly benign. But insofar as the fisherman and his wife represent the human predicament—in its contingency on forces beyond knowing, in its fearfulness and also its courage—the Ramsay dwelling is analogous to the pigsty by the sea.

The full range of worldly positions coveted and momentarily held by the fisherman's wife—from pigsty to Vatican—point to the representative function of the Ramsays. They are neither poor nor rich, powerful nor powerless; in them is the possibility of all human weakness and strength. To domineer is a human tendency. In Sir William Bradshaw, the psychiatrist in

Mrs. Dalloway, this tendency had become a mono-mania: "he shut people up," domineering in order to isolate them. In Mrs. Ramsay, the tendency was quite the opposite: she brought people together. It was, as Lily remembers, "part of her perfect goodness."

Her husband performs a complementary function —which is not so apparent as that of his wife. Mrs. Ramsay's influence is so universally welcome and so benevolent that his less amiable contribution to the human circle is easy to overlook. Yet Woolf has provided significant indicators throughout the novel.

In part one, Ramsay's fight against "the dark of human ignorance" requires his wife's comforts and the support of heroic models from literature. In that part, in which Mrs. Ramsay's role as comforter and confidante to all is of first importance, "The Charge of the Light Brigade" is employed largely to show Ramsay in a comic light, thus magnifying the need for his wife's solicitude. But in part three, with his wife dead, a similar allusion to Cowper's "The Castaway" is used to extend Ramsay's role from *paterfamilias* to leader of his people. After his wife's death, Ramsay stands alone, which allows his sterner role, no longer obscured by her "perfect goodness" to be visible.

Some indication of this role shows in the genuine ambivalence toward Ramsay on the part of the three most prominent feminine characters—Lily, Mrs. Ramsay, and Cam. Mrs. Ramsay is frequently irritated by his tyrannical ways, but regards him as a great man struggling with the unknown powers. Lily sees him as the oppressor of his children's lives, but also as a leader, a thinker unwaveringly concentrated on something visionary and austere. And Cam, though in league with her brother James against Ramsay's tyranny, remembers how free one felt with him in his study, and in the boat "how she was safe, while he sat there."

James's feeling for his father is one of intense love-hate. As the six-year-old victim of Ramsay's "infallible" prediction that bad weather would cancel the expedition to the lighthouse, he "could have gashed a hole in his father's breast and killed him, there and then." Ten years later, though still smarting under the "tyranny" of his father, James arrives at a sense of identification with him as he realizes that they share a view of life as being "clear, sharp and hard." And, as Cam observes when Mr. Ramsay remarks "Well done!" on James's steering, that was what he wanted: "His father had praised him."

What these ambivalences point to is Ramsay's true role in the novel: he is generically Man, the leader of his People, the builder of empires and systems of thought, the lonely explorer of his world, the doubt-riddled man-child whose insecurity causes him to make ferocious demands on others. Underneath Ramsay's ludicrous striding up and down, muttering about someone's blundering in Crimea, was a core of conviction that in the larger human situation someone had always blundered and that, indeed, someone always would. Can a man in the work of his lifetime do anything to offset those blunders?

This was the question that drove Ramsay in his quest for certainty (one must always know the points of the compass) and completeness (if all knowledge is represented by the alphabet, and one has reached the letter Q, one must struggle on to reach R.) Sitting in the middle of a small boat dolefully intoning "We perished, each alone," makes of Ramsay a superficially comic picture of a man. But Lily, hearing these words spoken by Mr. Ramsay in the morning before he sets out in the boat, feels that "the words became symbols, wrote themselves all over the grey-green walls." Cowper's poem did indeed provide Ramsay with a text that represented his prevailing mood of doubt and agnosticism: the sailor, washed overboard in a storm and left to drown by his captain, who dared not risk the ship by turning back, was like any man in a crisis abandoned to his own resources.

To the Lighthouse may be read as an elegy on the warmth of Mrs. Ramsay's character and as a tribute to the power of art represented by Lily Briscoe's completed painting: perhaps, too, a commemoration of the view of life held by both—"curled and whole like a wave." But it is also another of Virginia Woolf's intensive explorations of the mysterious male-female interplay—and perhaps formally the most satisfying. For it does not rely on rhetorical statement and counterstatement as in *Night and Day* but on fully realized dramatic situations. Only in the extravaganza that follows *To the Lighthouse, Orlando,* are the possibilities more ingeniously—and more blatantly—developed.

6

◇◇◇

Orlando
and
The Waves

*I'm sick to death
of this particular self.
I want another.*

The idea for *Orlando* took root in Virginia Woolf's imagination within a single hour in 1927—to sketch in a "grand historical picture" the outlines of all her friends. She puzzled over "how to do it" until she hit on writing it as "a biography," beginning in the sixteenth century and continuing to the present day. Orlando would be its hero-heroine, changing from one sex to the other.

The sexual metamorphosis was partly for fun—it appealed to her carefree mood. It was partly a way of dramatizing her view that life is whole and that the best men have something of woman in their makeup. And it was partly too—perhaps the larger part—to create in Orlando a fictional character to match the feminine charm and masculine force of her confidante, Vita Sackville-West, whose photographs, representing her as "Orlando," appear in the original edition. She formed the whole novel in plot and style to give the playful, fantastic tone of the masques, allegorical entertainments, that she wrote for intimates. She described the style as something like her personal letters with everything tumbled in pellmell.

But the surface playfulness of *Orlando* only partly camouflages a serious concern for the ideas expressed. The fantastic plot of the novel (a summary of which follows) has a diversionary function similar to that of the style: it is a scintillating, sometimes gaudy cover for Virginia Woolf's investigations into the serious matters of self and sex (both sexuality and gender), life and death, man and nature.

Orlando, born in the sixteenth century into a wealthy family, develops literary ambitions. He has written a closet full of derivative poetry—epic and dramatic. Presented to Queen Elizabeth, he is shortly afterward taken into the court, where he becomes a lover to the queen. In London he also meets Sasha, a Russian princess. After a torrid relationship, Sasha is faithless and sails back to Muscovy, after which Orlando falls into a long trance, the first of several that occur at critical points in his life.

He awakens to remember little of his past. It is now the reign of Charles II, and Orlando, near thirty (though historical time has moved half a century) is appointed an ambassador to Constantinople and elevated to a dukedom. He continues to write, is married overnight to a gipsy dancer, Rosina Lolita, and during a sack of the city falls into another trance from which he awakens metamorphosed into a woman. The transformation is announced via dancers in a masque, in which Our Ladies of Purity, Chastity, and Modesty are driven from the scene by Truth—which is Woolf's fanciful satire on the whole capricious enterprise of *Orlando*.

Returning to England as a woman, Orlando has difficulty proving her legal right to lands and title, but takes up again her neglected poem, "The Oak Tree," goes into London society, meets prominent literary figures of the eighteenth century, and seeks out an evening of "honest conversation" with prostitutes. This episode, one of several vicarious wish fulfillments, originated in Woolf's envy of her friend and rival Katherine Mansfield's ability to consort easily with the demimonde. Orlando also encounters Nicholas Greene, an eighteenth-century critic whom she had known as a literary hack in the time of Shakespeare. If Greene represents the critic Edmund Gosse, as Quentin Bell surmises, Woolf allows her malicious pen to score him in each of four centuries.

In the nineteenth century, still a young woman, Orlando finds herself more languishing and romantic, as befits the temperament of that moist century. She encounters Marmaduke Bonthrop Shelmardine, a wealthy landowner, who nevertheless spends most of his time at sea. This dashing creature is a male embodiment of Vita Sackville-West, once described by Virginia as a splendor of "candle lit radiance, stalking on legs like beech trees, pink glowing, grape clustered" —and other such extravagances. The legal question of Orlando's title to land is settled favorably, and she marries Shelmardine.

Into the twentieth century, she bears a son and has her poem published through the good offices of Sir Nicholas Greene, now a professor and successful literary critic. The narrative stops abruptly at the present moment: "midnight, Thursday, the eleventh of October, Nineteen hundred and Twenty Eight."

Fanciful this certainly is, but the final effect, as she hoped in projecting the novel, is of both "fantasy and truth." The underlying seriousness of several themes is not to be reduced even by Woolf's own occasional references to "joke" and "farce": she gives her usual intense scrutiny to the search for identity, including sex and marriage, death, and the relationship between man and nature. But catching herself on the verge of offering homilies, she observes that such "moralities belong, and should be left to the historian, since they are as dull as ditch water." Instead, she presents them in the delightful narrative tradition of Ovid's *Metamorphoses*, allowing the fantastic changes to occur in a matter-of-fact way.

Especially like Ovid is the motif of sexual change: "Different though the sexes are, they intermix. In every human being a vacillation from one sex to the other takes place." The Theban prophet Teiresias represents the association of sexual change with prophetic power.

Forced to live the life both of man and woman, and blinded to the outer world, Teiresias received in compensation the gift of inward sight. To see into the inner life of man or woman and to move freely through that territory of the "common life which is the real life," was Virginia Woolf's compensation for occasional insanity and for exclusion from the masculine world of affairs.

Her gift enabled her to establish a voice in her fiction—human yet prophetically detached—like that of the controlling point of view, also represented to be Teiresias in Eliot's *The Wasteland*. This point of view gave her, as it did her friend Eliot, the confidence to explore behind the outward lives of her characters to discover their motivations and compulsions, a confidence manifest in the tone of prophetic authority reverberating through her next novel *The Waves*.

Despite its capriciousness, *Orlando* is a substantial work of fiction. The impressionistic rendering of three centuries of English manners and literary history would alone give it a permanent interest. But in addition, it offers felicities of style, delights of parody, and thematic subtleties that remain the undisputed territory of ingenious readers, criticism having so far neglected to give this novel serious attention. If it suffers in comparison with *The Waves*, Virginia Woolf, at least, recognized both as legitimate expressions of her creative energy—*Orlando* her need to play on the surface, and *The Waves* her compulsion to dive and explore the depths.

She saw these two aspects of her writing as providing a creative dialectic that would allow her art to retain its tension without breaking—one kind of book relieving the other. After *Orlando*, she wanted to "dive" again. But, fearful of losing the spontaneity and

directness that had taken her so long to gain, she devised a new concept that would exclude everything that
did not belong to the moment: "Why admit anything
to literature that is not poetry—by which I mean satu-
rated?"

Consequently, a reader should not expect to find
in *The Waves* an arrangement of material in which one
event clarifies what has just preceded it. The object of
style in this novel is not clarification but enrichment—
of suggestion, of connotation, of correspondences between nature and human nature. For these reasons *The
Waves* is the most "poetic" of Virginia Woolf's novels
—not that these enrichments are not also abundant
elsewhere but that here she exploits them.

The Waves is divided into nine sections of soliloquies, each section preceded by a short group of itali-
cized paragraphs referred to here as preludes. The nine
stages in the daily course of the sun evoked in the
preludes are connected with nine stages in a fifty-year
span of human life in the soliloquies—beginning with
dawn in nature and with children in the nursery.
Human effort and defiance are set "against time and
the sea." The two patterns of rise and fall—that of
nature, and the surge and subsidence of human effort
—are parallel in each prelude and soliloquy: in the
first prelude, the fledglings in the garden leave their
nest, in the first soliloquy section, the children leave
home to go away to school.

Characterization through soliloquy calls for atten-
tive reading, but the seven personalities presented are
surprisingly well delineated through the changes of fifty
years. The following summary suggests the individuality of characterization but does not attempt to approach the complexity or interrelationships.

Bernard is the major figure, whose long soliloquy

concludes the novel. Virginia Woolf first conceived of Bernard as a woman and a writer. Whatever reason she had for changing the gender, Bernard remains a writer in her final conception, and manifestly her alter ego. He lives by words and believes in the reality of language: "When I cannot see words curling like rings round me I am in darkness—I am nothing." His earliest significant act in childhood is to follow Susan when he sees her crying, in order to comfort her. Yet he interprets his compassion and his need for an audience as failings; he believes that his character is not "authentic" because of his reliance on the stimulus of other people. Early in life he formulates a sense of human solidarity: "I do not believe in separation. We are not single." But he is aware, from observing his own children, that differences are sharp and persistent. It is he who finally unites in himself the separate powers of isolation and community to exemplify the defiance of passivity and the defiance of death central to the novel.

Susan is the only one of the women to marry and have a family. She is possessive, desiring only her farm, her children, her animals—and despises London for having nothing to do with these. She is elemental, like something in nature. Louis thinks of her as having "the stealthy, yet assured movements . . . of a wild beast." Her emotions are intense and undivided: "I hate, I love." She thinks sometimes that she is not a woman, but the light, or the seasons, or mud, or mist. Her primitivism merges with domesticity. She returns from a walk through the fields and woods, like a cat or fox, and then bakes bread, prepares meat, makes the kettle boil, and sews. She embodies maternal energy and singlemindedness. As Bernard represents the intellectual life force, Susan represents the physical. This op-

position is underlined by their attitudes toward language: Bernard lives by words, Susan hardly knows
that language exists: "The only sayings I understand
are cries of love, hate, rage, and pain."

Percival is a presence throughout the novel,
though he does not have a soliloquy of his own. Until
section five he is, living, an influence on the thoughts of
the other six, and thereafter, though dead, a vital
memory in their minds. He is the spirit of Virginia
Woolf's brother, Thoby Stephen, who, like Percival,
died in his mid-twenties. Leonard Woolf, a friend of
Thoby's at Cambridge, described the aspect of his
character that went into Percival: "there was a magnificent and monumental simplicity in Thoby which
earned him his nickname of The Goth." Percival has
none of the fear or vanity of the others; to them he is a
superior being. When he is among them they all become "sober and confident," like soldiers before their
captain. Bernard imagines the people in India clustered
around Percival "regarding him as if he were—what
indeed he is—a God."

Jinny lives for society, and in the moment. Her
responses are instinctive to the overtures of bodies—
the appraising looks of women, the inviting looks of
men. When most people are preparing to go to bed, for
Jinny the night is just beginning: "I am arrayed, I am
prepared . . . This is my calling. This is my world." It
is a particular London world, consisting of gilt chairs,
servants, and flowers. She passes through that world in
a series of liaisons, committing herself wholly to each
one. As she says of her numerous lovers: "My body
goes before me, like a lantern down a dark lane . . . I
dazzle you; I make you believe that this is all." To her
it *is* all. Her commitment makes a thematic statement,
like her own character, "hard and clear as crystal."

Approaching old age, aware that her charms are fading, she is defiant. Bernard observes: "When the lock whitened on her forehead she twisted it fearlessly among the rest."

Rhoda, Louis, and Neville are the remaining three. They are solitaries—"renegades," as Bernard sees them, because they want to set up separate existences. For Rhoda, life is a monster that emerges from the sea. She does not believe that one moment leads to another: "To me they are all violent, all separate . . . I have no end in view." By "no end" she means one person or idea—she has no confidence even in the reality of herself. She does not see herself as having so much as the substance of a wave—she is like foam flung on the beach. Since Rhoda is unable to draw on either personal courage or the strength of human solidarity, her suicide is predictable, and her own self-analysis a suitable epitaph: "I trust only in solitude and the violence of death."

Louis for a while is Rhoda's love. He often feels hatred and bitterness for Bernard and Neville because they are the sons of gentlemen and he is an alien, his father a failed Australian banker. Bernard and Neville have inherited money and position while Louis, "the best scholar of the lot," must pore over shipping documents in an office. Louis's resentment permits his intelligence to lapse into hypercriticism. He hates the others, except Susan and Percival, because it is for them that he sees himself performing the antics of smoothing his hair and concealing his accent. Thus Louis (like Rhoda, though for other reasons) cannot command the resources of companionship. This inability, however, seems to strengthen his commitment to imposing order on the disorderly world that he sees around him. But it is a lifeless commitment without

human attachments, and he appears true to his "fig-
ment" in Bernard's imagination—sculpturesque, a figure of stone.

Neville, the third of the solitaries, is "scissor-cut-
ting exact." For Neville, the glorious life would be "to
addict oneself to perfection." He objectifies that perfection in Percival, using him as the impossible measure
for all men: Louis is "acrid, suspicious, domineering,
difficult"; Bernard, knowing everybody, "knows no-
body." Neville's quest for the glorious life of perfection
is impeded by his desire to be loved and famous. His
quest narrows to a search for the perfect beloved, that
is, one who will love him perfectly. Unlike Jinny's liaisons, which are the result of her capitulation to the
body's instinctive responses, Neville's are the result of
his intellectual passion for perfect union. Since these
relationships can never be perfect and are therefore
always transitory, he is (like Rhoda and Louis) deprived
of the sustaining warmth of companionship. In his
loneliness, though, he is persistent and courageous: "I
am never stagnant; I rise from my worst disasters. . . ."
And he does, except for one: his commitment to
perfection.

The same may be said of all these men and
women (except for Percival), for they display the
characteristic alternating action of the waves: the fall
into passivity and disintegration, and the resurgence
into defiance and form. Even Rhoda, who at the nadir
of her despairing self-knowledge, thinks of herself as
foam on the beach, resists her despair to assert, "I am
also a girl here in this room." Resistance may be seen
to run in ascending effort from Jinny and Susan to
Bernard, and in progressive disintegration from Louis
and Neville to Rhoda. The balance, however, is on the
side of resurgence.

Woolf's use of the sea demonstrates her concern for the integrity of her writing: "One wants some device which is not a trick." The sea is such a device, as it surges and ebbs on the beach and in the minds of the six characters. The soliloquies are another such device, permitting the interflow of the characters' identities so that when they speak, they speak not just for Bernard or Rhoda or Jinny—they speak for the human condition.

By the time Virginia Woolf came to the last stage of writing *The Waves*, she tossed aside all the symbols so carefully prepared, using them "simply as images, never making them work out; only suggest." But the original preparation of images and symbols, making it possible for her to toss them aside (her way of describing it in the diary), was very careful indeed. The images in each prelude are emblematic of events in the soliloquy section that follows—the images of surfeit, for instance. In the sixth prelude, the birds "paused in their song as if glutted with sound, as if the fullness of midday had gorged them." In the following soliloquy, Susan, sitting by her baby, thinks how her veins are filled with life, until, moving about her tasks, she wants to protest, "No more, I am glutted with natural happiness." Even in part nine, where by her own account Woolf was letting the symbols work underground, the parallels are evident between images in the prelude and images in the soliloquy section. In the prelude, the leaves of a tree are described falling to the ground. "There they settled with perfect composure on the precise spot where they would await dissolution." And in the soliloquy section Bernard meditates, as his hair falls to the floor in the barber shop, "So we are cut and laid in swathes . . . so we lie side by side on the damp meadows, withered branches and flowering." These correspondences are not simply verbal, as they may seem when deprived of context and the support of cumulative detail. Rather they are essential to the formal relationship between prelude and soliloquy in the nine parts.

Mortality appears to dominate in the course of the nine preludes, as the energy of the sea, visible in the waves, batters down everything. In prelude after prelude its destructive power intensifies, though in prelude seven there is a lull. Beneath the lull, the sea is gathering the power that in prelude eight becomes a great wall of water toppling over the land. Prelude nine describes the coming night as being like waves washing everything over in primeval darkness.

But a countermovement is developed in resistance to this power, a countermovement against death that is the central theme of *The Waves*. In a diary entry, Woolf stated that "the theme Effort, Effort dominates: not the waves." It is clear that from the beginning she meant to establish a persistent struggle between human will and the great impersonal forces of nature. The struggle is dramatically unequal, but Woolf reduces the odds in two ways.

The first is to borrow the idea of the sea for her human protagonists: the sea is not only "out there," a force in the external world, but "inside" as well, the source of psychic energy and imaginative power. It is the ancient concept that the mind, like the sea, includes all things—and so includes the sea. In this respect, the imagery of Neville's self-analysis is revealing:

I am immeasurable; a net whose fibres pass imperceptibly beneath the world. My net is almost indistinguishable from that which it surrounds. It lifts whales—huge leviathans and white jellies . . . I detect, I perceive.

The consequence of this marine duality in nature and in man is that the rise and fall of nature's power, as represented by the sea, is paralleled in the rise and fall of resistance to that power in the internal worlds of the characters, especially Bernard. At the end, standing in the street as day breaks, Bernard thinks, "Yes, this is the eternal renewal, the incessant rise and fall and rise again. And in me the wave rises."

Thus nature in the preludes is shown increasingly to exercise a power that is indifferent to man and that may possibly overwhelm him. Man in the soliloquies is represented as vulnerable but defiant, and through the development of mind and imagination, daring even to challenge that power.

The second way Virginia Woolf equalizes the struggle between individual human force and the impersonal force of nature is through the time-defying, death-defeating power of art. Percival is "a hero"—he inspires poetry—and the fact that he dies before his deeds flower does not impair his inspirational function. His deeds are only hypothetical in the minds of his admirers—they believe that had he lived he would have "saved India," he would have "done justice," at forty he would have "shocked the authorities." At the end, when the "wave rises" in Bernard, it is Percival with whom he identifies himself. He remembers him as the hero on horseback. Taking Percival as his model, Bernard conceives of himself as striking spurs into his horse and riding against Death. For Bernard, Percival has become one in the "long ranks of magnificent human beings," and Bernard is the inheritor, the continuer, "the person miraculously appointed to carry on." Thus Bernard properly invokes his spirit in the challenge to mortality.

Though he has not been successful as a writer,

Bernard has much of the character of the writer as
artist. He lives by words; when words are not "curling
in smoke" around him, he is "in darkness," he is nothing. He needs an audience. He is chameleon-like in
assuming the personalities of Tolstoy, Byron, or Mere-
dith—"I am this, that, or the other." But chiefly he is
the artist in that when there is something in him to be
expressed, he is under compulsion to say it. He is
driven with a "moth-like impetuosity dashing itself
against hard glass." So, in the last section, when he
meets a slight acquaintance going into a restaurant,
Bernard is compelled like the Ancient Mariner to tell
him his story. But Bernard is designedly not a hero and
not the successful artist. He is meant to stand for any
human in whom the wave of resurgent vitality can rise
and fall. And though death is the human equivalent to
the breakdown of waves into the impersonal synthesis
of the sea, Bernard is defiant.

The theme—the celebration of imaginative vitality—is most powerfully illustrated in the intense poetic
form of the novel itself, the nine parts structured like
large, complex stanzas, forming a great ode. In this
lengthy elaboration of her theme, Virginia Woolf has
done for the ode what Hopkins did for the sonnet in
"Spelt from Sibyl's Leaves"—enlarged, extended, and
packed the original form far beyond its traditional di-
mensions, while retaining the dialectical force of its
structure in statement, counterstatement, and synthesis.

Five words conclude the novel in a brief epode:
The waves broke on the shore. They recall Rhoda's
feeling that she was only foam on the beach ("a wave
that broke"). But she had also reacted against that
feeling of personal disintegration with, "I am also a girl
here in this room." Virginia Woolf, herself defiant, as-

serted her claim to be "curled and whole like a wave" through the death-defying form, curled and whole, of *The Waves.*

The brief epode contains the germ of the novel and should not be read in isolation from the rest. Though it contains no explicit human reference, the human element is there through the structural linking of all the epodes back to the first, where the waves breaking on the shore are described as *sighing like a sleeper whose breath comes and goes.* Thus the final epode, the last line of the novel, does not signal the defeat of man simply because he is not mentioned: asleep, he is gathering forces to resist. The epodes carry the theme that is the synthesis of all the statements and counterstatements making up *The Waves*: process matters, not conclusion, and human Effort rises perpetually, and as mysteriously as sleep, to the challenge.

7

◇◇

The Years
and
Between the Acts

*. . . the book of the world turned back
to the very first page.*

Bernard, in *The Waves*, is very much the artist Virginia Woolf, who throughout her life, as many diary entries indicate, identified herself with a rider on horseback, taking her leaps gallantly, riding against death. In none of her works was she to set herself a larger challenge than in undertaking to write her next serious novel, which was to be published in 1937 as *The Years*.

Divided into eleven chronological periods by dates—1880, 1891, 1907, and so on to the last, titled "Present Day"—*The Years* is an account of three generations of the Pargiter family. Colonel Pargiter has seven children, of which Eleanor, in her early twenties as the account begins, figures most prominently. The Colonel's brother, Digby, has two daughters, of whom Sara, still a child in 1880, has a part in the story comparable in importance to Eleanor's.

A prelude introduces each chronological period, indicating the season. It sets the tone for the section to follow through a description of the weather. The end of the prelude to 1880 suggests that the novel is panoramic: "Slowly wheeling, like the rays of a searchlight, the days, the weeks, the years passed one after another across the sky." But despite the fact that sixteen more or less active characters are taken through three generations from 1880 to 1935, the effect of the novel is better described as visionary.

This is attributable largely to the pursuit of a tranquil inner life that receives extended development in the final section of the novel, comprising a third of its total length. In this section, Eleanor Pargiter expresses her desire to attain tranquility through enclosing the present moment, "to make it stay; to fill it fuller and fuller, with the past, the present and the future, until it shone, whole, bright, deep with understanding."

Aspirations of this kind, expressed in rather vague language, gave currency to the opinion that Woolf's writing was an "idealized, romantic fantasy of what should have been." She hoped that sticking to "facts" would save her from the rarified theorizing of such as the Cambridge don, Goldsworthy Lowes Dickenson: "Goldie depresses one unspeakably. Always alone on a mountain top asking himself how to live, theorizing about life; never living . . . and never notices a face or a cat or a dog or a flower, except in the flow of the universal." And by "facts" she meant not only natural beauty and the attractive varieties of faces, cats, dogs and flowers but also the skeleton beneath the flesh— the sordid as well as the pleasing.

For Woolf took an essentially realist position that this was the given mixture of the external world. Her objective was not to deny one order of "facts" (the sordid)in order to idealize the world through the other order of "facts" (the pleasing). She wanted to describe the world as it is in its mixture of the ugly and the beautiful and to accept that mixture. "Vision" was what she called the reconciliation of these two kinds of facts. *The Years* was to be a book about a world of both fact and vision: "I mean, *The Waves* going on simultaneously with *Night and Day*." This objective allows for the deformities, perversions and falsehoods that show as facts of life in the representative world of *The Years*, and the final acceptance of the world as it is in the novel's tranquil conclusion.

The world of the Colonel Abel Pargiter family in 1880 is a world of hypocrisy, deception, perversion, deformity, disease, and death. Mrs. Pargiter is confined to her bed in a terminal illness. The Colonel (retired) paws at his mistress with a crippled, clawlike hand. The youngest daughter, Rosie, is accosted under a lamp post by a pervert. The older Pargiter children, psychologically depleted by their mother's long illness, try to conceal from themselves and each other their guilty wish that she would get done with dying. We see the other branch of the Pargiter family, whose servants, Colonel Pargiter observes, are "Italian dagoes." This ethnic ugliness is in the pattern of remarks about the "Jew from Birmingham" in the Cambridge section. In the Digby Pargiter family, we also see Sara who, dropped in babyhood, now has a crippled shoulder. When Sara's middle-aged parents die, a Pargiter remarks how terrible old age is and how fortunate they are to die in their prime. But on another occasion another Pargiter remarks on what awful lives children lead and, she adds, they can't tell anyone.

This dark chronicle of the years is balanced by intermittent appearances of beauty and glimpses of meaning. In the present these are manifest in effects of weather and the glittering surface of things. The song of the pigeons (which Eleanor hears as "Take two coos, Taffy, take two coos") would appear to be a minor effect except that its deliberate overtones of domesticity and sharing of creature comforts persist and become associated with marriage, family ties, and civilization. To the ends of beauty and meaning Woolf also utilizes the arts—painting from time to time and literature throughout.

Sophocles's *Antigone*, for example, though used primarily by Woolf to recall the fate of the stubbornly principled girl immured alive for her rebellion against the state, is also a powerful example of self-knowledge. Eleanor, going over an obituary notice about her uncle Digby Pargiter, thinks, "But he wasn't like that. . . . No, not like that in the least," and puts down the obituary to go on with her reading in Renan's *Life of*

Jesus. What is the truth about a man named Jesus, about what he said under a fig tree that was written down by another man? Suppose what that man wrote is "just as false as what this man . . . says about Digby?"

Yet here she is, "getting a little spark from what someone said all those years ago." Antigone, Jesus, Shakespeare, Parnell—all are "mysterious" personages, from whose lives one may receive an intimation about one's own ambiguous self here and now—what the pattern of his particular life is and what the larger pattern of life itself might be.

Many such attempts to discover patterns establish the structure of *The Years*. From the beginning, the story moves from an outer world of observed facts, disconnected and confusing, toward an inner vision that provides a glimpse of pattern in the facts. Such a movement characterizes the narrative—from its uneasy, fragmented opening to the tranquil conclusion, and several of the larger episodes imitate this movement, so that the novel seems in retrospect not at all episodic but whole and integrated.

Virginia Woolf's diary records the special significance that one of the larger episodes had for her: how she wrote and rewrote to make "each sentence" express its "great pressure of meaning." It involves a sequence of events on one afternoon beginning at Saint Paul's Cathedral and concluding, as though in some calm center of meaning, at the Round Pond in Kensington Gardens.

It is a beautiful spring day in London in 1914, and Sara, slightly crippled and eccentric, has arranged to meet her married sister Maggie in late afternoon. She unexpectedly encounters her bachelor cousin Martin outside Saint Paul's. They have lunch, after which they go together to meet Maggie.

The 1914 world described by Woolf is as full of hypocrisy, deception, and ugliness as the world of 1880 with which the novel began. In the restaurant where Martin and Sara have lunch, conversation is difficult—"it is broken into little fragments." As they leave the restaurant, Martin is angry because the waiter had tried to cheat him. Conversation in the street is impossible; the street is too narrow, there are crowds, the traffic is noisy. As Martin bends over a woman selling violets, he sees that her face has been mutilated by some disease. They try to walk, but carts, newspaper boys, men and women get in their way, so they are obliged to take a bus down Piccadilly toward Hyde Park Corner.

The journey of Martin and Sara across London moves them from confusion and ugliness toward tranquility at the Round Pond. Sara is the first to feel the change as the beauty of the day affects her, and she gazes with rapture at the sun blazing on windows. Inside Kensington Gardens, as they walk toward the Round Pond, Martin also falls under the spell of the beautiful afternoon. The dappled sunlight gives everything a look of transparency, and Martin discovers that he too seems "dispersed" in this setting of "primal innocence." They meet Maggie with her baby at the Round Pond, and Sara falls asleep on the grass while Martin and Maggie talk about babies, Martin's love affairs, and shared memories of the two Pargiter families.

Martin has undergone more than a simple trip by foot and bus across town to a pond in the park: he experiences a moment of tranquility and a sense that life may not be so disconnected and inimical as he had thought. Having chosen the company of Sara out of boredom with himself, he has gone step by step with her toward a feeling of increasing intimacy. At the Pond, while Sara sleeps, his feeling is transferred to Maggie as he confides his troubled emotional life to her.

But Martin is not left in this euphoric condition, for Woolf is true to her thesis that vision does not permanently reshape life in ideal forms but only imparts momentary meaning, a glimpse that leaves the visionary better able to cope with the world's mixture of the beautiful and the ugly. Martin, having reached tranquility with himself and companionship with his cousin Maggie, watches two toy boats nearly collide on the waters of the pond, reminding him of the world of "fact" and its perils. Resuming his conversation with Maggie about love and family, he is again recalled to the world of "ordinary proportions" when his laughter wakens Maggie's baby, who begins to cry: "Their privacy was over. The child cried. The clocks began striking."

These moments of balance between the inner and outer worlds occur to several of the Pargiters. But Eleanor appears as the protagonist in that she embodies the search for self-knowledge more extensively than any other, and in "Present Day" achieves a memorably described reconciliation with a reality in which "facts" are often sordid, inexplicable, or deadening. Eleanor's reconciliation is remarkably like that of Clarissa in *Mrs. Dalloway*: it occurs on a beautiful day in spring, late in the course of a large party attended by family and friends; it involves her recognition that human understanding is limited, that love has many forms, that isolation is death, and companionship means life.

Eleanor gropes toward these ideas from early in the novel, but from "1911" on to "Present Day"

(1935), they take on more explicit shape. In "1911,"
in bed late at night, Eleanor is reading Dante. She is
sleepy and the Italian is hard: ". . . the meaning escaped her. There was a meaning, however." She turns
to the translation: "For by so many more there are
who say 'ours'/So much the more of good does each
possess." The meaning still eludes her, and becoming
more sleepy she puts out the candle. "Darkness
reigned." The meaning of Dante's lines about human
solidarity has only brushed her mind, and for this time
is lost as darkness takes over.

   In "1917," Eleanor is at a dinner party with
Maggie and Maggie's French husband Renny, her
cousin Sara and Nicholas, an exotic foreigner and
overt homosexual. There is an air raid, during which
they take shelter in the basement. After the air raid, as
Eleanor is preparing to leave, all her mixed feelings
about Nicholas—of repugnance and fascination—have
come together in liking. She goes to the window, sees
the stars, and has a "sense of immensity and peace—as
if something had been consumed. . . ." She is unable to
account for her feelings, but remembers Maggie and
Renny sitting over the fire and decides that what she
has been feeling all the time was a happy marriage. As
she leaves the house, a searchlight still sweeps the sky:
"It seemed to take what she was feeling and to express
it broadly and simply, as if another voice were speaking in another language."

   Though Eleanor is moved by something to her
indefinable, a reader of *The Years* will sense that the
"something indefinable" has to do with the varieties of
human relationships—that of the exotic Nicholas with
the volatile Sara, of Maggie with her pacifist French
husband, of both couples with Eleanor, and (as a result of the air raid) of them all with the "enemy."

The vignette that closes the "1917" section of the novel illustrates human relationship at the most general level of casual contact. On the bus, Eleanor finds herself staring unconsciously at an old man who is eating something out of a paper bag. He catches her looking, and "cocking one eyebrow over his rheumy, twinkling old eyes," asks if she would like to see what he has for supper, holding out for inspection a piece of meat and bread. Woolf takes us in less than a page from Eleanor's meditation on the larger pattern of things to her encounter with mundane particularity in the little old man and his sandwich. The juxtaposition of vision with fact makes its point, and the chapter ends.

Not until many years later (in "1935") does Eleanor attain the understanding that enables her to make the symbolic gesture on which the novel so tranquilly concludes. In the course of the party at her sister Delia's house, Eleanor passes through several stages of self-questioning to arrive at a state of peace with herself, with her relatives, and with the hitherto obdurate world of unmanageable facts. Eleanor comes to accept, even to understand, the relationship between her crippled cousin Sara and Nicholas, instead of simply tolerating it, as in the past. Though these two would appear to be unlikely candidates for a lasting relationship, they have been inseparable for years. Eleanor, overhearing their bickering and laughter at the party, perceives that this is their love-making: "They are aware of each other; they live in each other."

As the party begins to break up, just before dawn, Eleanor tries to complete her vision in the present moment, to make it stay, full of the past, present, and future, "deep with understanding." She has to admit, instead, that it is useless. Night would give way to "the endless dark." And as she thinks of death, trying to visualize that endless dark, dawn breaks, lightening the room.

The enigma of a world that evaded Eleanor's comprehension—its light and dark, its beauty and ugliness—confronts her again in the caretaker's two children brought in by Delia to sing for the company. The words of their song are unintelligible to the listeners, their voices shrill and discordant. Eleanor is struck by the contrast between their faces and their voices— how dignified they looked, yet how hideous the noise they made. She wonders if it is possible to find one word for both impressions, for the whole—perhaps "beautiful?"

This idea of the beautiful as something mixed, or even incongruous, is reinforced as Eleanor observes the statuesque appearance of her tired, overweight relatives in evening dress silhouetted against the fresh light of morning, and as she hears the crooning of the wood pigeons in the trees overhead ("Take two coos, Taffy, take two coos"). The meaning of certain things that Eleanor had puzzled over, reading Renan ("God is love, the kingdom of Heaven is within us, sayings like that"), are now apparently clear. A sense of her own responsibility for what happens—new beginnings, new possibilities—is crystalized in her mind by the sight of a young man and woman across the street leaving a cab and going into a house. As the door closes on them, she turns to her brother Morris to signal her own new beginning: "And now?" she asks, "holding out her hands to him. The sun had risen, and the sky above the houses wore an air of extraordinary beauty, simplicity and peace."

This conclusion might appear to confirm the characterization of Woolf's writing as idealized and romantic, except that she had already balanced it, shortly before the conclusion, by a significant reservation. It is embodied in the toast Nicholas had prepared: He had been first going to thank his host and hostess, then their house "which has sheltered the lovers, the creators, the men and women of good will." And finally, he had been "going to drink to the human race . . . which is now in its infancy, may it grow to maturity!" Through Nicholas's lukewarm estimate of human progress, Woolf reduces Eleanor's vision to just a possibility that mutual sympathy and love might protect against personal isolation and a meaningless existence.

With her own vision thus balanced between skepticism and hope, Virginia Woolf undertook her last novel, *Between the Acts*. The precariousness of man's lot, his struggles to reconcile the parts of his divided self and his infrequent success, his attempts at union with other beings and the failure of communication that usually frustrates his attempts—to these motifs from *The Years*, Woolf returns in *Between the Acts*, where she incorporates the pageant of epochs, the pageant of centuries, and the pageant of years into the human pageant of a single day.

Between the Acts did not receive final revision before publication in 1941. Relatively brief (56,000 words—little more than a third the length of *The Years*), it is a complex, though superficially simple story. Even a surface reading, however, involves the reader in an intricate structure of relationships: male and female, love and hate, mankind and beasts, rationality and vision, art and nature, and life and death. Some idea of how they interrelate can be obtained from the following synopsis, though a sense of the allusiveness and intricacy of their combinations requires the full expression of the poetic, spare prose that is the final achievement of Virginia Woolf's art.

The story relates the events of twenty-four hours in the summer before the outbreak of war in 1939, centering on a village production of a pageant of English history, and involving three generations of a family named Oliver who occupy Pointz Hall: old Bartholomew Oliver and his widowed sister Lucy Swithin, Giles Oliver (son of Bartholomew), Giles's wife, Isabel, and their two children. The story begins on a summer night as the Olivers are talking with Haines, a gentleman farmer, and his wife.

During the evening, Isabel indulges in the fantasy of an erotic relationship between herself and Haines that will be balked, she foresees, by her husband Giles. Mrs. Haines, too, is aware of the emotion that excludes her, and in the car going home "she would destroy it, as a thrush pecks the wings off a butterfly." These emotional crosscurrents are set in the long perspective provided by old Oliver's comments about the history of the neighboring land—the still visible scars on the countryside made by the Britons, Romans, Elizabethans, the plow marks where wheat had been grown during the Napoleonic wars.

In bed next morning, the elderly Lucy Swithin reads an outline of history describing an age when rhododendron forests covered what is now Piccadilly. She is transported in imagination back among the iguanodons, "from whom presumably, she thought, we descend." The scene following, involving the little Oliver boy and his grandfather, returns from rhododendron forests to a moment in the present so intense that everything but the immediate experience disappears. The boy is in the childhood stage of primary identification with the world around him. He is in the garden looking at a flower that

filled the caverns behind the eyes with light. All that inner darkness became a hall, leaf smelling, earth smelling, of yellow light. And the tree was beyond the flower; the grass, the flower and the tree were entire. . . . Then there was a roar and a hot breath and a stream of coarse gray hair rushed between him and the flower. Up he leapt, toppling in his fright, and saw coming towards him a terrible peaked eyeless monster moving on legs, brandishing arms.

The child is frightened by his grandfather pretending to be an animal, and as he bursts into tears the grandfather goes off muttering that the boy is a crybaby. In these early scenes, Woolf establishes the conflict between the sexes, the brevity of human existence, and the intensity of experience in the present moment, that proliferate and combine intricately in the rest of the novel.

At lunch, the Olivers are unexpectedly joined for lunch by a Mrs. Manressa and William Dodge, a quiet and "ambiguous" companion. Mrs. Manressa, who keeps a country house in the district, has brought Dodge from London to see the pageant of English history to be produced in the afternoon as a benefit for the local church. Later during an intermission in the pageant, he is taken on a tour of the house by the gallant old lady, Lucy Swithin. She understands the cause of his turmoil and responds to him not as a half something but as a complete human being. As they walk through the upstairs rooms, Dodge is moved by her natural treatment of him almost to confide that she has "healed" him. But he is unable to move his feeling beyond thought into words, and so is not healed, is still a "half man"—just as anyone, Woolf implies, who does not signal his human impulses by some word or sign gives way to the "wild horse" in his nature and is consequently only half man.

William Dodge stirs an irrational dislike in the determinedly male Giles:

A toady; a lickspittle; not a downright plain man of his senses; but a teaser and twitcher; a fingerer of sensations; picking and choosing; dillying and dallying; not a man to have straightforward love for a woman. . . .

Giles is an unwilling businessman who, given his choice, would have farmed, and his frustration and resentment smoulder in every corner of his life. Mrs. Manressa sees something "fierce and untamed" in Giles, who is also upset and angry about the deteriorating conditions in Europe. Mrs. Manressa is earthy, spontaneous, and uninhibited. At the point in the pageant where "The Present" is dramatized by a parade of mirrors held facing the audience, she is the only one to gaze frankly at herself while the others avert their eyes in confusion; she knows who she is.

The writer and producer of the pageant is Miss La Trobe, who lives in alternating states of exaltation and despair, depending on how the audience receives her words: had she "made them see? . . . a vision imparted was a relief from agony." Her pageant presents a rambling miscellany of episodes from English history that has only a limited success in "making them see." As the Reverend Streatfield remarks: "Speaking merely as one of the audience, I confess I was puzzled. For what reason, I asked, were we shown these scenes?" But "these scenes" have moved Lucy Swithin, who approaches Miss La Trobe and "laying hold desperately of a fraction of her meaning," tries to communicate her feeling: "what a small part I've had to play! But you've made me feel I could have played Cleopatra." What she meant was, Miss La Trobe thinks, "You've stirred me in my unacted part."

Lucy, who has been moved by the pageant to think about human destiny, looks into the fish pond: " 'Ourselves,' she murmured . . . she followed the fish; the speckled, streaked and blotched; seeing in that vision beauty, power and glory in ourselves." Her faith contrasts with her brother's rationality: "He would carry the torch of reason till it went out in the darkness of the cave. For herself, every morning, kneeling, she protected her vision."

Miss La Trobe, meanwhile, has lost her momentary feeling of success; she had given but the giving was over: " 'A failure,' she groaned," and leaves for the pub to solace her loneliness and pride. As she drinks, she remembers a flock of starlings that had descended on a tree after the pageant, and how "the tree became a rhapsody, a quivering cacophony" of birds voicing discordantly "life, life, life without measure." As the memory floods her imagination, she sets down her glass, and inspiration taking over her mind, she hears the "first words" of her next creation.

A similar manifestation of the energizing power of nature occurs when the pageant appears about to collapse in silence—the gramophone will not play, actors forget their lines, vitality seems exhausted. But cattle on the hillside near the scene of the pageant erupt into spontaneous bellowing, and brute nature saves the occasion: "It was the primeval voice sounding loud in the ear of the present . . . bridged the distance; filled the emptiness and continued the emotion."

That evening, the pageant over and dinner through, "the Olivers come together in the big room as if for refuge, watching the night close in over their sheltering roof. It is the same room where they sat the evening before, and in this final scene the major themes of conflict again appear. Giles buries himself in some business letters, old Oliver in the newspaper, and Lucy returns to her outline of history: "Prehistoric man, half-human, half-ape, roused himself from his semi-crouching position and raised great stones." Isa tries to sort out her feelings about her husband, admitting that she both loves and hates him: "Love and hate—how they tore her asunder! Surely it was time someone invented a new plot, or that the author came out from the bushes. . . ." Isa and Giles, left alone in the room as the others go off to bed, find that enmity is bared.

The love-hate oppositions are interconnected throughout the novel: Isa's erotic fantasy about Haines, the ambiguity of her feelings for Giles, "the father of her children," Giles's instinctive male hatred of the "half-man" Dodge, and his equally instinctive attraction to the earthy Mrs. Manressa. Dodge's self-hatred, which arrives at the verge of being "healed" by Lucy's understanding and acceptance, has a bearing on old Oliver's mixed feelings about Lucy, who is so different from himself. She, in turn, fears and resents the jokes old Oliver cracks at her expense, so that their life together continues in the pattern of conflict set in their childhood, represented by the flower chains Lucy made and the bloody gills of the hooked fish Bartholomew caught. In Miss La Trobe the love-hate conflict works through the alternate feelings of contempt for her failures and adoration for her creative self. Finally, in the scene between Giles and Isa that concludes the novel, love-hate is shown as a primitive, almost elemental relationship, in which fighting and embracing prepare for the curtain to rise on the next act in their life.

The conflicts encompass oppositions both in man

and in nature. The divided self, in search of identity, is frustrated attempting to find clues in an external world whose principles of organization are apparently indecipherable. As Bart Oliver, the rationalist, asks himself,

why, in Lucy's skull, shaped so much like his own, there existed a prayable being? . . . It was, he supposed, more of a force or a radiance, controlling the thrush and the worm; the tulip and the hound; and himself, too, an old man. . . .

But the dualities of male-female, love-hate, and so on, are not always polarized. Virginia Woolf preferred the concept of process, which implies indeterminacy: man stands in relation to raw nature on a scale of involvement that moves between primeval ooze and the intricacies of language.

The imagery linking man to animals constantly reminds us of the relationship between them. Lucy, looking at the fish in the pond and considering their variations, murmured "Ourselves." The cattle breaking into the static moment of the pageant with their bellowing, linked "the primeval past to the present." The starlings, with their elemental joy in "measureless" life, triggered the creative mood in Miss La Trobe as she sat slumped in despair.

Of the many conflicts, that between imagination and reality produces the most tension, since it is the sensitive area of Virginia Woolf's own struggle to create believable fiction about a real world: "to make them see." Lucy Swithin embodies this crucial conflict in her feminine role as a visionary balancing Bart Oliver's practical male way of knowing. Her remark, "you've made me feel I could have played . . . Cleopatra" points up Miss La Trobe's power to evoke a reality through language.

She, like Virginia Woolf, lives only for her art: when the action grinds to a halt as the wind muffles the actors' lines, she groans in despair, "it's death, death"; but when the inspiration is upon her she, like the starlings, experiences "life, life measureless." If she is not creating, she is nothing. So Virginia Woolf, as Isa and Giles are about to quarrel and then embrace, also evokes through language another wave of reality, that flows on after the novel ends.

Allusions to speaking—the importance of verbal communications of all kinds—and the consequences of failing to speak, appear at several earlier points in the narrative. Yet, two of the creative moments result from energy expressed in wordless animal sounds—the cows' bellowing when the pageant begins to fall apart, and the starlings' clatter as they flock in the tree. What case is Virginia Woolf trying to make here for the "word"? First, that there exists a mysterious connection between the limited human mind struggling to create and the enormous reservoir of creative energy in nature. And second, that words can describe the connection so convincingly that we believe it.

She does not always succeed in this high objective. The reason may lie in E. M. Forster's remarks (in *Aspects of the Novel*) about "prophetic" fiction, that it "gives the sensation of a song or of sound . . . it flows athwart the action and the surface morality like an undercurrent. It lies outside words." Part of Woolf's achievement is to create an effect that does go beyond words.

The reader, of course, wants both the words and the music, as did Woolf herself, observing in *Jacob's Room* that she did not care for songs without words. What Woolf calls "vision" corresponds to Forster's "prophecy," and creation of the prophetic "song" or "sound" confronted her with the final duality and un-solvable dilemma of her writing.

Perhaps the last scene of the novel both expresses and embodies her dilemma. Giles and Isabel, just before going to bed, are alone together for the first time that day. They are silent.

Alone, enmity was bared; also love. Before they slept, they must fight; after they had fought, they would embrace. From that embrace another life might be born. But first they must fight, as the dog fox fights with the vixen, in the heart of darkness, in the fields of night.

Isa let her sewing drop. The great hooded chairs had become enormous. And Giles too. And Isa too against the window. The window was all sky without colour. The house had lost its shelter. It was night before roads were made, or houses. It was the night that dwellers in caves had watched from some high place among rocks.

Then the curtain rose. They spoke.

With that scene, the title "Between the Acts" assumes a larger significance. What is it that people do between the acts of the pageant, that is, the acts of their daily life? The novel richly demonstrates that what they do is largely instinctive, and energized by very primitive sources. They are themselves primitive, like the dog fox and the vixen, like the fish identified by Lucy as "ourselves."

Woolf reiterates in this kind of sophisticated animal fable what Nicholas in *The Years* stated in his toast—that the human race is in its infancy. And as the words of the children's song in *The Years* is unintelligible, so largely are the words of adults in *Between the Acts*. Even the words of the pageant frequently become unintelligible.

This is not to imply that Woolf's conclusion is a despairing one, but only that she recognized the formi-

dable task confronting even disciplined language to
make sense of the natural world and human motivation. The ordinary speech of ordinary people in ordinary circumstances—like that of Giles and Isabel—
expresses primitive needs. Only by making incessant
demands on language can words be made to assert
human control and enlarge the borders of civilization.
In the frame of Nicholas's metaphor about mankind
being in its infancy, the child must learn to speak.

This idea lay behind Virginia Woolf's own incessant struggle with words. Yet she was aware of a danger, a danger implied in the metaphor of mankind as
an infant. The child has a quality of fresh observation
and sources of inspiration that he loses as he acquires
knowledge and develops his rational outlook. And in
that dilemma of human maturation, Woolf recognized
the dilemma of the artist: how to maintain the vivid
freshness of the child to the advantage of an art that
required order, analysis, abstraction, and the conscious
manipulation of language? Forster's remarks provide a
clue: prophetic fiction gives a sensation of song that
lies outside words. It is not an answer, of course, but
neither is it an evasion.

To someone engaged in the action of life, one of
Virginia Woolf's novels, for instance, is something between the acts. Reading it, he feels, like Lucy watching
the pageant, that some unacted part of himself has
been aroused. There may indeed be a silent land, as
Virginia Woolf herself asserts, into which words cannot go. If that silent land is experience so vivid and
immediate that words cannot capture it, she would
capitulate to the impossible and say, as she so often
did, it's life, only life, that matters.

But we need to be reminded that only life matters,
and that is what art does. It enables us to live again

youth's voyage out, to view at a safe distance the struggle of light and dark in human nature, to participate in Orlando's healing fantasy, and to rise again out of defeat in the upward curve of the wave. Virginia Woolf created her fiction, to lie in this salutary way between the acts of life.

Notes

Chapter 1

The biographical material in chapter one is based in the main on Noel Annan's *Leslie Stephen*; Quentin Bell's *Virginia Woolf*; J. K. Johnstone's *The Bloomsbury Group*; *Recollections of Virginia Woolf*, edited by Joan Russell Noble; Leonard Woolf's *Autobiography*; Virginia Woolf's *A Writer's Diary*; *Virginia Woolf and Lytton Strachey: Letters*, ed. by Leonard Woolf and James Strachey.

1. Bell, *Virginia Woolf*, I, p. 61n.
2. "Mr Hudson's Childhood" in *Contemporary Writers*, p. 94.
3. "Leslie Stephen," *Collected Essays*, IV, p. 80.
4. *Beginning*, pp. 25–26.
5. "The Mark on the Wall," in *A Haunted House*, p. 45.
6. See "Virginia's Death" in Leonard Woolf's *Journey*.
7. *Journey*, p. 130.
8. See L. Woolf, *Downhill*, pp. 143–148.

9. Lehmann, *Whispering Gallery*, p. 169.
10. Plomer, in Noble, *Recollections*, p. 97.

Chapters 2–7

All quotations are from the work under discussion. Others not identified in the text are from *A Writer's Diary*. In addition, p. 80 contains a quotation from a letter in the Berg Collection, quoted by Quentin Bell in *Virginia Woolf*, II, p. 117, and p. 95 contains a quotation from George Rylands, in *Recollections of Virginia Woolf*, edited by J. R. Noble, p. 144.

Chapter epigraphs

1. Introduction to "Catalogue of Recent Paintings by Vanessa Bell."
2. *A Writer's Diary* (Hogarth), p. 57.
3. *Ibid.*, p. 65.
4. *Mrs. Dalloway* (Modern Library), p. 224.
5. *The Voyage Out* (Hogarth), p. 145.
6. *Orlando* (Hogarth), p. 279.
7. *The Voyage Out* (Hogarth), p. 206.

Bibliography

1. Works by Virginia Woolf

The Voyage Out, novel. London: Duckworth, 1915. New York: Doran, 1920. New York: Harcourt Brace, 1926.

The Mark on the Wall, story. Richmond: Hogarth Press, 1917.

Kew Gardens, story. Richmond: Hogarth Press, 1919.

Night and Day, novel. London: Duckworth, 1919. New York: Doran, 1920.

Monday or Tuesday, short stories. Richmond: Hogarth Press, 1921. New York: Harcourt Brace, 1921.

Jacob's Room, novel. Richmond: Hogarth Press, 1922. New York: Harcourt Brace, 1923.

Mr Bennett and Mrs Brown, essay. London: Hogarth Press, 1924.

The Common Reader, essays. London: Hogarth Press, 1925. New York: Harcourt Brace, 1925.

Mrs Dalloway, novel. London: Hogarth Press, 1925. New York: Harcourt Brace, 1925. (The Modern Library edition, 1928, has an introduction by Virginia Woolf.)

To the Lighthouse, novel. London: Hogarth Press, 1927. New York: Harcourt Brace, 1927.

Orlando: A Biography, fiction. London: Hogarth Press, 1928. New York: Crosby Gaige, 1928. New York: Harcourt Brace, 1929.

A Room of One's Own, polemic. London: Hogarth Press, 1929. New York: Fountain Press, 1929. New York: Harcourt Brace, 1929.

On Being Ill, essay. London: Hogarth Press, 1930.

The Waves, novel. London: Hogarth Press, 1931. New York: Harcourt Brace, 1931.

A Letter to a Young Poet, essay. London: Hogarth Press, 1932.

The Common Reader: Second Series, essays. London: Hogarth Press, 1932. New York: Harcourt Brace, 1932.

Flush: A Biography, fiction. London: Hogarth Press, 1933. New York: Harcourt Brace, 1933.

Walter Sickert: A Conversation, essay. London: Hogarth Press, 1934.

The Years, novel. London: Hogarth Press, 1937. New York: Harcourt Brace, 1937.

Three Guineas, polemic. London: Hogarth Press, 1938. New York: Harcourt Brace, 1938.

Reviewing, essay. London: Hogarth Press, 1939.

Roger Fry: A Biography. London: Hogarth Press, 1940. New York: Harcourt Brace, 1940.

Between the Acts, novel. London: Hogarth Press, 1941. New York: Harcourt Brace, 1941.

The Death of the Moth, and Other Essays. London: Hogarth Press, 1942. New York: Harcourt Brace, 1942.

A Haunted House, and Other Short Stories. London: Hogarth Press, 1944. New York: Harcourt Brace, 1944.

The Moment, and Other Essays. London: Hogarth Press, 1947. New York: Harcourt Brace, 1947.

The Captain's Death Bed, and Other Essays. London: Hogarth Press, 1950. New York: Harcourt Brace, 1950.

A Writer's Diary, selections. London: Hogarth Press, 1953. New York: Harcourt Brace, 1954.

Virginia Woolf and Lytton Strachey: Letters. London: Hogarth Press and Chatto & Windus, 1956. New York: Harcourt Brace, 1956.

Granite and Rainbow: Essays. London: Hogarth Press, 1958. New York: Harcourt Brace, 1958.

Contemporary Writers, reviews. London: Hogarth Press, 1965. New York: Harcourt Brace Jovanovich, 1965.

Collected Essays, 4 volumes. London: Hogarth Press, 1966–67. New York: Harcourt Brace Jovanovich, 1966–67.

Nurse Lugton's Golden Thimble, children's story. London: Hogarth Press, 1966.

NOTE: For a nearly complete listing see A *Bibliography of Virginia Woolf*, compiled by B. J. Kirkpatrick (New York: Oxford University Press, 1968, second edition).

2. Works about Virginia Woolf

BIOGRAPHIES

The authorized biography is Quentin Bell's *Virginia Woolf*, published in 1972 in England by the Hogarth Press in two volumes, and in the United States by Harcourt Brace Jovanovich. An earlier biography by Aileen Pippett, *The Moth and the Star* (Boston: Little, Brown & Co., 1955), contains previously unpublished material. Twenty-seven "recollections by contemporaries" have been edited and introduced by Joan Russell Noble, *Recollections of Virginia Woolf* (London: Peter Owen, Ltd., 1972). The most circumstantial account of Virginia Woolf's life after marriage appears in her husband's autobiography:

Leonard Woolf. *Sowing: An Autobiography of the Years 1880 to 1904*. London: Hogarth Press, 1960.

―――. *Growing: An Autobiography of the Years 1904 to 1911*. London: Hogarth Press, 1961.

―――. *Beginning Again: An Autobiography of the Years 1911 to 1918*. London: Hogarth Press, 1964.

―――. *Downhill All the Way: An Autobiography of the Years 1919 to 1939*. London: Hogarth Press, 1967.

―――. *The Journey Not the Arrival Matters: An Autobiography of the Years 1939 to 1969*. New York: Harcourt, Brace & World, Inc., 1969.

CRITICISM: BOOKS

Bennett, Joan. *Virginia Woolf: Her Art as a Novelist*. 2nd edition. Cambridge: Cambridge University Press, 1964.

Blackstone, Bernard. *Virginia Woolf: A Commentary*. London: Hogarth Press, 1949.

Brewster, Dorothy. *Virginia Woolf*. New York: New York University Press, 1962.

Chambers, R. L. *The Novels of Virginia Woolf*. Edinburgh: Oliver & Boyd, 1947.

Daiches, David. *Virginia Woolf*. Norfolk, Conn.: New Directions, 1942.

Guiguet, Jean. *Virginia Woolf and Her Works*. Translated by Jean Stewart. New York: Harcourt, Brace & World, 1965.

Hafley, James. *The Glass Roof: Virginia Woolf as Novelist*. English Studies, No. 9. Berkeley: University of California Press, 1954.

Holtby, Winifred. *Virginia Woolf*. London: Wishart, 1932.

Leaska, Mitchell. *Virginia Woolf's "Lighthouse": A Study in Critical Method*. New York: Columbia University Press, 1970.

Love, Jean. *Worlds of Consciousness: Mythopoetic Thought in the Novels of Virginia Woolf.* Berkeley: University of California Press, 1970.

Marder, Herbert. *Feminism and Art.* Chicago: University of Chicago Press, 1963.

Moody, A. D. *Virginia Woolf.* New York: Grove Press, 1963.

Nathan, Monique. *Virginia Woolf.* Translated by Herma Briffault. New York: Grove Press, 1961.

Rantavara, Irma. *Virginia Woolf's "The Waves."* Helsingfors: Societas Scientiarum Fennica, 1960.

Richter, Harvena. *Virginia Woolf: The Inward Voyage.* Princeton: Princeton University Press, 1970.

Schaefer, Josephine. *The Three-Fold Nature of Reality in the Novels of Virginia Woolf.* The Hague: Mouton & Co., 1965.

Woodring, Carl. *Virginia Woolf.* New York: Columbia University Press, 1966.

CRITICISM: ARTICLES, COLLECTIONS,
AND PARTS OF BOOKS

NOTE: For detailed listings see Maurice Beebe, "Criticism of Virginia Woolf: A Selected Checklist," in *Modern Fiction Studies*, II, 1 (1956), 36–45; and Jane Novak, "Recent Criticism of Virginia Woolf: January 1970–June 1972," in *Virginia Woolf Quarterly* I, 1 (Fall 1972).

Aiken, Conrad. "The Novel as a Work of Art" (*To the Lighthouse*) and "Orlando," in *Collected Criticism*. New York: Oxford University Press, 1968.

Auerbach, Erich. "The Brown Stocking." In *Mimesis*, translated by Willard Trask. Princeton: Princeton University Press, 1953.

Baldanza, Frank. "Clarissa Dalloway's Party Consciousness." *Modern Fiction Studies*, II (February 1956), 24–30.

————. "*To the Lighthouse* Again." PMLA, LXX (June 1955), 548–52.

Bazin, Nancy Topping. "Virginia Woolf's Quest for Equilibrium." *Modern Language Quarterly*, XXXII, 3 (September 1971), 305–319.

Beach, Joseph Warren. "Virginia Woolf." *English Journal*, XXVI (October 1937), 603–612.

Beck, Warren. "For Virginia Woolf." In *Forms of Modern Fiction*, edited by William Van O'Connor, pp. 243–54. Minneapolis: University of Minnesota Press, 1948.

Beja, Morris. "Matches Struck in the Dark." In *Epiphany in the Novel*. Seattle: University of Washington Press, 1971.

Bevis, Dorothy. "*The Waves:* A Fusion of Symbol, Style, and Thought in Virginia Woolf." *Twentieth Century Literature*, II (April 1956), 5–20.

Blotner, Joseph. "Mythic Patterns in *To the Lighthouse*." PMLA, LXXI (September 1956), 547–62.

Brace, Marjorie. "Worshipping Solid Objects." In *Accent Anthology*, pp. 489–95. New York: Harcourt Brace, 1946.

Brower, Reuben. "Something Central Which Permeated: Virginia Woolf and *Mrs. Dalloway*." In *The Fields of Light*. New York: Oxford University Press, 1951.

Cohn, Ruby. "Art in *To the Lighthouse*." *Modern Fiction Studies*, VIII (Summer 1962), 127–36.

Doner, Dean. "Virginia Woolf: In the Service of Style." *Modern Fiction Studies*, II (February 1956), 1–12.

Empson, William. "Virginia Woolf." In *Scrutinies II*, edited by Edgell Rickword, pp. 203–216. London: Wishart, 1931.

Forster, E. M. *Virginia Woolf: The Rede Lecture*. New York: Harcourt Brace, 1942.

Freedman, Ralph. *The Lyrical Novel: Studies in Hermann Hesse, Andre Gide, and Virginia Woolf.* Princeton: Princeton University Press, 1963.

Friedman, Norman. "The Waters of Annihilation: Double Vision in *To the Lighthouse.*" *English Literary History,* XXII (March 1955), 61–79.

Gelfant, Blanche. "Love and Conversion in *Mrs. Dalloway.*" *Criticism,* VIII (Summer 1966), 229–45.

Graham, John. "Time in the Novels of Virginia Woolf." *University of Toronto Quarterly,* XVIII (January 1949), 186–201.

————. "Point of View in *The Waves:* Some Services of the Style." *University of Toronto Quarterly,* XXIX (April 1970), 193–211.

Havard-Williams, Peter and Margaret. "Perceptive Contemplation in the Work of Virginia Woolf." *English Studies,* XXXV (1954), 97–116.

Hoffmann, Charles G. " 'From Lunch to Dinner': Virginia Woolf's Apprenticeship." *Texas Studies in Literature and Language,* X (Winter 1969), 609–627.

Hunting, Constance. "The Technique of Persuasion in *Orlando.*" *Modern Fiction Studies,* II (February 1956), 17–23.

Johnstone, J. K. *The Bloomsbury Group.* London: Secker & Warburg, 1954.

King, Merton P. "*The Waves* and the Androgynous Mind." *University Review,* XXX (1963), 128–34.

Leavis, F. R. "After *To the Lighthouse.*" *Scrutiny,* X (January 1942), 100–105.

Latham, Jacqueline E. M., ed. *Critics on Virginia Woolf: Readings in Literary Criticism.* Miami: University of Miami Press, 1970.

Mellers, W. H. "Virginia Woolf: The Last Phase." *Kenyon Review,* IV (1942), 381–87.

Miller, J. Hillis. "Virginia Woolf's All Souls' Day: The

Omniscient narrator in *Mrs. Dalloway.*" In *The Shaken Realist: Essays in Modern Literature in Honor of Frederick J. Hoffman.* Baton Rouge: Louisiana State University Press, 1970.

Novak, Jane. "Virginia Woolf—'A Fickle Jacobean.'" *Virginia Woolf Newsletter,* III (April 1972), 1–8.

Overcarsh, F. L. "The Lighthouse, Face to Face." *Accent,* X (Winter 1959), 107–123.

Pedersen, Glenn. "Vision in *To the Lighthouse.*" *PMLA,* LXXIII (December 1958), 585–600.

Proudfit, Sharon Wood. "Lily Briscoe's Painting: A Key to Personal Relations in *To the Lighthouse.*" *Criticism,* XIII (Winter 1971), 26–39.

Rachman, Shalom. "Clarissa's Attic: Virginia Woolf's *Mrs. Dalloway* Reconsidered." *Twentieth Century Literature,* XVIII (January 1972), 3–19.

Ramsey, Warren. "The Claims of Language: Virginia Woolf as Symbolist." *English Fiction in Transition,* IV (1961), 51–58.

Roberts, John Hawley. "Vision and Design in Virginia Woolf." *PMLA,* LXI (September 1946), 835–47.

Rosenbaum, S. P. "Philosophical Realism of Virginia Woolf." In *English Literature and British Philosophy,* edited by S. P. Rosenbaum, pp. 316–57. Chicago: University of Chicago Press, 1971.

Samuelson, Ralph. "Virginia Woolf: *Orlando* and the Feminist Spirit." *Western Humanities Review,* XV (Winter 1961), 51–58.

Savage, D. S. "The Mind of Virginia Woolf." *The South Atlantic Quarterly,* XLVI (July 1947), 557–73.

Schorer, Mark. "The Chronicle of Doubt." *Virginia Quarterly Review,* XVIII (Spring 1942), 200–215.

Sprague, Claire, ed. *Virginia Woolf: A Collection of Critical Essays.* Englewood Cliffs: Prentice-Hall, 1971.

Szladits, Lola L. " 'The Life, Character, and Opinion of

Flush the Spaniel.' " *Bulletin of the New York Public Library*, LXXIV (1970), 211–18.

Toynbee, Philip. "Virginia Woolf: A Study of Three Experimental Novels." *Horizon*, XIV (November 1946), 290–304.

Vogler, Thomas A., ed. *Twentieth-Century Interpretations of "To the Lighthouse."* Englewood Cliffs: Prentice-Hall, 1970.

Webb, Igor. " 'Things in Themselves': Virginia Woolf's *The Waves.*" *Modern Fiction Studies*, XVII, 4 (Winter 1971–72), 570–73.

Index

WITHDRAWN